THE STORY OF THE

Fender ®

Stratocaster

Ray Minhinnett & Bob Young

GPI Books
An Imprint of
mf *Miller Freeman Books*

First published in the United States in 1995 by Miller Freeman Books
600 Harrison Street, San Francisco, CA 94107
Publishers of GPI Books, *Guitar Player*, *Bass Player* and *Keyboard* magazines
A member of the United Newspapers Group

Distributed to the book trade in the U.S. by
Publishers Group West, P.O. Box 8843, Emeryville, CA 94662

Distributed to the music trade in the U.S. by
Hal Leonard Publishing, P.O. Box 13819, Milwaukee, WI 53213

ISBN 0-87930-349-2

Library of Congress Cataloging-in-Publication Data

Minhinnett, Ray
        The story of the Fender Stratocaster: curves, contours and body horns:
        a celebration of the world's greatest guitar / by Ray Minhinnett &
        Bob Young
            p.   cm.
            Includes discographies
            ISBN 0-87930-349-2
            1. Stratocaster – History.   2. Stratocaster – Construction
3. Electric guitar – History. I. Young, Bob, 1945- . II. Title.
            ML 1015. G9M56 1995   94-33586
            787.87' 1973 – dc20   MN

Project Editor: Tessa Rose
Technical Editor: Paul Trynka
Project Art Direction: Fiona Knowles
Designer: Bobbie Colgate Stone
Production: Garry Lewis

Printed and bound in Spain

95 96 97 98 99 5 4 3 2 1

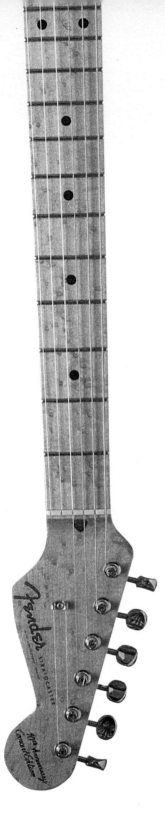

CONTENTS

CURVES, CONTOURS AND BODY HORNS

Jimi Hendrix

Leo Fender's Stratocaster is far more than just an electric guitar. The standard cliché would be to say that it is an icon, but it is much more than that. Whereas icons, such as Levi jeans or Wurlitzer jukeboxes, reflect or evoke history, the Stratocaster made history. Without the Strat, as it is affectionately termed, it is doubtful whether Buddy Holly, Jimi Hendrix, Eric Clapton and a host of influential blues and country musicians would have been able to articulate the sounds they heard in their heads, and rock music would consequently have sounded very different.

Eric Clapton playing the original 'Blackie'

The idea for *Curves, Contours and Body Horns*, a film about the world's most influential guitar, was born early in July 1992 when Ray was at home working on a new song. It took only a few hours to complete a 25-page blueprint. The two of us had often talked about setting up a TV production company, and it was obviously a God-given opportunity when eventually *Curves* was accepted as a TV special. Bringing the story of the Strat to the screen, and indeed to the following pages, has been both a labor of love and a nightmare of logistics and political maneuvering.

The Stratocaster has probably been the subject of more good old yarns than any other musical instrument. When we set out to make a film, and then write a book, about its influence, we suspected that musicians would want to talk about the guitar that was essential to their work, but if anything we underestimated their eagerness. If you're an Eric Clapton or Keith Richards you're more likely to be asked about the most obscure details of your personal history than to be asked about your guitar playing; yet it was the electric guitar that put Eric and Keith where they are today. To musicians, the electric guitar fulfils a huge variety of roles, from that of a security blanket – something to hold or hide behind when thousands of pairs of eyes are watching you – to that of a faithful collaborator with whom, at the right times, you can reach places no-one else can reach. Whatever the

1961 Stratocaster: it still looks contemporary

other distractions surrounding their careers, for many guitarists their life's work is a search for that ultimate sound, that ultimate note, and for all of the guitarists interviewed in this book, the Stratocaster was an integral part of that search. The metaphors used are endless: to Keith Richards, the Stratocaster is the sniper's rifle which complements his short-range Sten gun, the Telecaster. To Eric Clapton the Strat is a vehicle which embodies

Buddy Holly and the Crickets

his own personality, which over time he can imbue with his own character. To Bryan Adams it's something solid which stops him feeling exposed when he's standing in front of a micro-phone. That's pretty good going for a simply made instrument designed by a small group of Californians in 1954.

To us, the story of the Strat is a vital part of the history of the 20th century. The shape and function of the electric guitar are now utterly familiar – ask anyone in the street to draw one

Eric Clapton

and it's likely that the outline will be derived from that of the Strat. Yet in 1954 the look of the Strat was something devastatingly new, completely divorced from any guitar that had gone before. Leo Fender and his colleagues seemingly ignored all of instrument-making

history when they designed it, recognizing that dispensing with the conventional guitar shape and construction would make a more versatile, hard-wearing instrument. The Strat, like its predecessor the Telecaster, provoked mainly bemusement when it first appeared. Over the years, however, its qualities became more and more obvious, to the point where today it's fair to say that it's the best electric guitar that has ever been designed. Modern electric guitars which don't borrow a few tricks from the Strat are exceedingly rare – modern electric guitars which go all out to copy it are exceedingly common.

Yet along with their technical genius, the Strat's designers built in a bit of magic, too. George Harrison compares the Strat to the Chrysler Building as a symbol of the 20th century; Jeff Lynne compares it to the finest Picasso, while countless others compare it to the Stradivarius, the legendary violins conceived in 17th-century Cremona, Italy. Some onlookers have accused the solid electric guitar of having no craftsmanship, no resonance, and no character. The fact that the Strat wasn't a product of expensive woods and traditional craftsmanship does not affect its position as a masterpiece, however. Like the Stradivarius the Strat was an inspired solution to a set of technical problems, and like the Stradivarius, the Strat is a product of its own time: 20th-century America, the cradle of mass production and capitalism. It couldn't have been built in any other place, or in any other period, and the cast of characters who participated in its success also evoke Fifties Americana.

As with any legendary invention, the story behind the Stratocaster is a complex one; 40 years on, there are varying accounts of how it came about. At the center of the story is Leo Fender, a non-musician and fanatical engineer, who after a business lunch was quite likely to crawl underneath a car in the street to check out its suspension. There was Freddie Tavares, a skilled draftsman whose Hawaiian-guitar playing can still be heard on the *Loony Toons*

cartoon theme. There was George Fullerton, a shy Fullerton resident who was Leo Fender's

first assistant, and production manager Forrest White, who kept Leo Fender in order, and who

is more likely to call a spade 'a bunch of crap' than a spade. Bill Carson was the man who

soaked up the ridicule as he field-tested early versions of the Strat, while Don Randall, the

charismatic salesman with movie-star looks, had to go out and sell it – no easy task. There are

tales of Fender salesmen pushing shop-owners up against walls to sell early shipments, while

Leo Fender himself was prone to exasperate his salesmen by giving the guitars away. Despite

Filming Dick Dale for Curves, Contours and Body Horns

the problems, those responsible for the

Stratocaster always believed it was going to

be a success. The fact that it became a legend

was more of a surprise, and there are now

many who claim to have played an integral

part: as Don Randall says, 'success has a thou-

sand fathers'. Industrial historians could also

take lessons from the Stratocaster story,

which was the chronicle of a classic design which suffered from unsympathetic management

and foreign competition before being re-evaluated as a classic brand name.

Here, then, is the story of the most important musical instrument of the 20th century: how

it was invented, how it changed through the years, and how the world's musicians were won

over by it. If we've done our job properly, it should make you want to go out and play a

Stratocaster, or listen to one. Tell 'em Ray & Bob sent you.

RAY MINHINNETT

My love affair with the Fender Strat began in 1974, when I bought a 1959 sunburst maple neck Strat, serial number 35562, which had belonged to Steve Marriott. I finally had one! I paid $650 for it, and I've played it to this day. I think you need to be a guitarist or a guitar-lover to understand the passion that we feel for these instruments; it's a relationship for life. Hopefully the film Curves, Contours and Body Horns *and the book you are about to read will go some way in helping those of you who aren't guitarists to understand this emotional relationship, and teach you a lot of other things you didn't know about Leo Fender's Stratocaster – the guitar that gave us rock 'n' roll.*

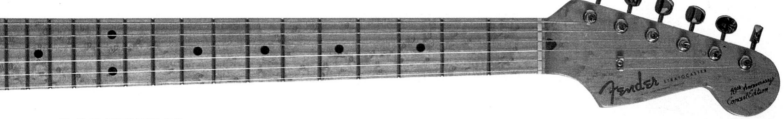

BOB YOUNG

Tracing the story of the Fender Strat was like completing a giant jigsaw puzzle. There was a huge wish list of people we wanted to interview, and while there were those who thought we were being over-ambitious in trying to collect together such a unique and illustrious group of artists, there were thankfully one or two people who believed we could write, produce and deliver a film on Leo Fender's finest invention. Out of our film have sprung concerts, an album, an extended program, various other offshoots and, of course, this book, which we hope will appeal to everyone, players and non-players – in fact, anyone who enjoys a good story. We've been helped hugely by a diverse group of players, Fender employees and others whose lives have been touched by the Strat. Hopefully, this book will help you to appreciate the magic of one of the most beautiful, original and influential inventions of our time.

CHAPTER ONE

THE EARLY YEARS

Many self-styled electronics inventors set up shop in the postwar United States – few would

be as successful as Leo Fender. In a few short years inventions such as the Telecaster and

Precision Bass revolutionized the music industry and paved the way for the Stratocaster.

Above: Leo Fender
Right: The Fender
factory was a regular
haunt for many
country musicians.
Here Leo Fender
(second right) poses
with a group including
Brother Oswald (far
left), Shot Jackson
(second from left) and
Roy Acuff (center)

When Leo Fender established his electric guitar and amplifier company in postwar California, the United States was in a uniquely productive phase. Electronics, TV and radio broadcasting, all of which had arrived before the war, rapidly increased in importance as the country tooled up for a consumer revolution. Leo Fender, like many other potential inventors tinkering with electronic circuitry in their backyard sheds, saw the application of electricity to the guitar as an exciting

growth area. But even he would be genuinely staggered by the influence his inventions would come to exert.

Clarence Leo Fender was born in a barn near Anaheim in Orange County, California, in 1909. His parents were farmers and, as he recalled later, the barn was their only accommodation at the time: 'There were horses on the east side, a hay mound in the center, and we lived on the west side. Eventually, by 1910, the folks were able to

build a house.' The young Leo took a couple of years of piano lessons before switching to saxophone, but would never lay claim to any competence as a musician. Instead, his first employment was as an accountant with the State Highways Department. After four years, with the advent of the Depression, Leo found himself jobless.

'I remember at one time things were very hard. I managed to get a day job but in order to get by I was also taking on radio repairs. At the same time I managed to get a portable PA system and I used to hire that out. Eventually I had three complete PA systems which were kept busy at athletics and sports events.'

Ultimately the PA hire business earned Leo sufficient capital to open The Fender Radio Service, a retail and repair shop on Spadra Road, Fullerton, around 1939. 'For the first few weeks I went from house to house looking for work. That lasted about three weeks. After that I had so much work I didn't ever have to go looking again.'

At the time Leo was building up his radio business, the electric guitar was starting to become established. Several manufacturers had brought electric instruments onto the market as early as 1929, but the instrument generally credited as the first production electric guitar was the Rickenbacker A-22, or 'Frying Pan', of 1932. This early electric guitar was in the lap steel configuration popular with Hawaiian and country guitarists at the time. Lap steel, or 'Hawaiian', guitars are placed on the

player's lap, and the strings are pitched by means of a steel bar or slider to give the smooth legato sound familiar from Hank Williams records or Hawaiian tunes such as "The Hawaiian Wedding Song". Lap steel guitarists were by far the biggest customers for those early electrics even though Rickenbacker and several other companies had produced electric guitars in standard or 'Spanish' guitar formats by the mid Thirties. Many players dismissed the electric guitar as a mere gimmick, particularly because the early instruments, such as Rickenbacker's solid Bakelite Electro Spanish B, didn't even look like conventional guitars. Even

The Bob Wills Band were the first to record with Fender guitars. Seen here with the Band's tour bus are: Billy Bowman (far left), Forrest White (middle) and Freddie Tavares (far right)

so, by 1936 industry heavyweights like Gibson weighed in with their own electric guitars, and by 1941 the company's archtop ES-150 electric had become well-known, thanks to the innovative electric jazz guitarist Charlie Christian. Christian and other guitarists, such as T-Bone Walker, started to give the electric guitar some credibility outside Hawaiian or country music circles. The instruments they played, however, were essentially old-fashioned hollow body models with a pickup stuck on. Other guitarists, wanting to be heard in noisy clubs or to cut through big bands, started to turn to the new instruments.

Leo Fender, a fan of the Western Swing and Hawaiian music formats which were the first to feature the electric guitar, was an early convert to the new sound. At that time California was a hotbed of electric guitar activity; electric pioneer Rickenbacker was based nearby in Los Angeles, Les Paul was working in Bing Crosby's California studio with his own solid body electric called 'The Log', while Paul Bigsby would build a pioneering solid body guitar for Merle Travis around 1947. One other electrical experimenter who would play a key part in the Fender history was Clayton Orr 'Doc' Kauffman, a violinist and lap steel player who had designed the snazzy Electro Vibrola guitar for Rickenbacker. Doc Kauffman became a regular visitor to Leo's shop during the Second

George Fullerton with '59 blonde maple neck Strat

World War, and the two soon began to work on electronic gadgetry together before setting up their own company, K&F (for Kauffman and Fender) in 1945, making lap steels and small amplifiers. Donald D. Randall, who would later become responsible for Fender's sales operation, still vividly remembers Leo's spirit of invention:

'My time with Leo goes back to around 1940. Leo had a small radio shop, and I had a small radio parts and equipment house – everything was small in

Fullerton at the time! Leo was repairing radios and I was supplying parts. We did a lot of business at the time and we struck up a pretty fast friendship. Then the War came along and I spent three years in the service; Leo didn't have to go in because he'd lost an eye in an accident when he was a kid, so he had a pretty thriving business. When I came out of the service I got talking with Leo and he said "You know Don, we really ought to build something," and I said "Yeah Leo, figure out what we can do." He came out with several items – one of them was a scratch polish remover you rubbed on mahogany or oak to get rid of the scratches – but that didn't go, and then he made a glue, that didn't work, but we eventually kind of migrated into the music field. He had a fellow called Ray Massey who started fooling around with amplifiers and got the country and western guys interested, then Leo's association with Doc Kauffman really made his interest peak. Doc only stayed a little while, but we built the guitar thing up from there.'

Although Doc Kauffman helped spark Leo Fender's interest in electric guitars, the joint K&F venture only lasted a few months – according to Doc, it was just too much like hard work: 'I just couldn't have stood it. Leo would go down at night, always be working. I wanted to be home with my kids at night, but I'd usually be in that shop until ten.'

George Fullerton, a local musician who met Leo during the war and would later become one of his closest associates, still remembers Doc suffering in the Fender workshop: 'Doc was a very fine musician . . . He'd spend a lot of time working on different guitar parts, or pickups, but I remember watching him one day working on a piece of equipment you use in metal die shops, a filing machine with an up and down vertical motion, and you had to hold the metal to be filed up against it. While Doc Kauffman was working with it, that machine would grab the piece of metal he was filing, and raise it up and drop it down again, and pinch blood blisters on the end of all his fingers.

He had to play that night with his group. I remember him saying that was one of the most difficult things he had to put up with, playing with blood blisters on every one of his fingers.'

Following Doc's departure, Leo – with typical economy – used up his stock of 'K&F' nameplates before naming his solo venture the Fender Musical Instrument Co. From now on he would concentrate on musical-instrument manufacture rather than the radio retail business, with his amplifiers and lap steels distributed by R&TEC (Radio and Television Equipment Company), owned by Francis Hall and run by Don Randall.

Around the time he was working with Kauffman, Leo Fender had started to experiment with his first solid body electric Spanish guitar. According to George Fullerton, 'Leo made one little guitar, glued the fretboard on a piece of wood, added a pickup and strings and one day he called me over to take a look at it – I played with a group and he wanted me to go out and test it. It was very good, except it was very small and hard to hold. That would have been around 1944/5.'

Leo later recalled that he would occasionally hire out that first prototype, but he was aware that something so basic was not ideal for commercial production. It would be 1948 before he started work on a fully-fledged attempt to make a commercial solid body guitar. The Fender company by now had a profitable line of lap steel models, while the amplifier business, which would always constitute an important sector of Fender's profits, was also helping to establish the company's reputation with local musicians. Leo's ambitions to produce a completely new instrument were by comparison a long shot, for there was no proof that a market existed. In fact, the close collaboration with musicians that would greatly benefit Fender arose primarily through trying to sell its early products, as George Fullerton recalls: 'In those days guitars weren't too plentiful, and neither were guitar players. With a new item, a solid body guitar, people weren't standing in line trying to buy them – to get them to see them meant taking them out to the

bandstands, and the only time we could do that was at night, when the bands were playing. So Leo would go out in many different directions in LA to locate a band and take something out for them to try out on the bandstand. This turned out to be a very effective way to test instruments, as well as introducing them to the public.'

While Leo was developing his ideas for the Broadcaster, other inventors, in particular Les Paul and Paul Bigsby, were also working along similar lines. According to George Fullerton, Leo was well aware of Bigsby's solid electric, which in certain ways would resemble the Broadcaster: 'Leo was interested in solid body guitars maybe before Paul Bigsby, but he wasn't too far along in

This early Fifties catalogue heavily emphasizes Fender's new solid body electric

Eldon Shamblin visits the Fender factory in 1957. Raymond Earl, a Western swing player who, like Shamblin, had worked with Bob Wills, is about to restring Shamblin's guitar.

designing them in those early days, 'cause he was busy working in the retail shop and repairing radios. Paul Bigsby built more than one guitar for Merle Travis, and I'm sure that at different times he showed it to Leo, and Merle showed it around too, so I'm sure it was an influence to Leo to get something going on his own.'

Perhaps Bigsby did influence Leo to an extent, but it would certainly not be Bigsby who put the solid electric guitar on the map. That required an inventor who thought in terms of mass production and would also have the skills to market such a radically new instrument.

THE BIRTH OF THE BROADCASTER

From his work on lap steels, Leo was aware that a solid body electric guitar could give a purer, more sustained sound with less susceptibility to feedback. His vision for this new instrument would bring the Broadcaster into being. As with all of his subsequent designs, Leo's work on this new instrument went through several prototypes as he tested out different pickups and control configurations. By early 1950 his design was ready for mass production. Some early fliers featured an initial one-pickup version of the guitar known as the

Esquire, but Fender's Broadcaster, so named by Don Randall to tie in with the modern age of electronics and broadcasting, was Fender's first production Spanish electric. It was also one of the most significant milestones in the history of popular music.

To say Leo Fender's radical new instrument created a stir on its launch would be more than an exaggeration – it would be an outright lie. Most onlookers regarded the new instrument with complete bemusement. Even Fender's distributor, R&TEC, which had been enjoying a healthy income from Leo Fender's lap steels and amplifiers, was distinctly underwhelmed by this unfamiliar, and thus hard-to-sell, creation. For this reason much of the original sales material and marketing effort came from Fender itself, which bypassed R&TEC to sell many of its new instruments directly. To make matters worse, Don Randall's name for the new guitar was already in use by the Fred Gretsch company who had a drum kit named Broadkaster. Pressure from Gretsch forced Fender to come up with a new name: once again Don Randall obliged, titling the instrument the Telecaster.

The guitar would, of course, become famous under that name, and remain in production basically unchanged to this day. Leo Fender had got almost everything right, despite the Telecaster being his first stab at making a modern electric guitar. Although traditionalist dealers at first balked at the new instrument, it soon won a hard core group of fans among musicians.

In 1950 Leo Fender's Telecaster was staggeringly unusual. All the other electric guitars on the market were hollow body archtop instruments with added pickups. Designed as an electric from the ground up, the Telecaster was uncomfortably austere by comparison. To its competitors the Telecaster was totally devoid of craftsmanship, and more akin to a canoe paddle or a breadboard. Industry heavyweights such as Gibson and Gretsch derided this weird Californian creation, but within a matter of a couple of years they would all be working on their own versions.

Practically every element of the Telecaster was unique. First was its solid body, a simple slab with a single cutaway, usually made from two finely matched pieces of ash. Although the likes of Paul Bigsby had made one-off solid electrics, Leo's design was unique in production terms. Second, its all-maple bolt-on neck was made from one piece of wood with the frets inserted directly into it. Fender's rivals used necks with separate finger-boards, and the necks were glued into the body – the Telecaster's bolt-on construction radically simplified mass production and repair of the instrument. Third, its stamped steel bridge assembly allowed for adjustment of string height and intonation; rival manufacturers used separate bridge and tailpieces made of wood, which usually offered little room for adjustment.

There were countless other innovations: a radical stripped-down headstock design which presented all the tuning pegs in an easy-to-get-to line, and whose 'straight string pull' offered improved tuning stability by avoiding having the strings kink or splay out at the nut; two distinctly voiced pickups which could be easily selected via a sliding switch; a modular design which had all the wiring mounted on a steel plate, screening the electronics. Every one of these innovations represented a real improvement over the guitar's archtop predecessors and, more importantly, the instrument sounded good, too.

In developing the Telecaster, Leo Fender instinctively adopted concepts that would become cardinal principles in electric guitar design, concentrating on obtaining a rigid structure which would give good definition and sustain. Leo's explanation of the thinking behind the Tele was typically straightforward: 'We were trying to get a tone like you get with the steel guitar, because a steel was so much cleaner in sound than an acoustic. We wanted to have something that you could hear that had sustain and a lack of feedback. It's a stronger instrument than an acoustic. Musicians can use them in a club in a fight if they

The Fender Telecaster, launched as the Broadcaster, was the world's first significant solid body production electric. This example dates from 1952

have to. If you get clobbered over the head with one of those, you know you've been hit!'

Although Don Randall encountered indifference to Fender's new instrument, within a few months it had won some exalted endorsees, including country star Jimmy Bryant. George Fullerton remembers his use of the Telecaster as a major turning point: 'The first time he played one, all his group stopped playing to watch him and all the audience crowded round. The rest of the group didn't get back on the bandstand for that entire evening. He became the first professional musician to play the Fender guitar.' Although Fender and its new-fangled ideas had been initially dismissed as the products of California weirdos, its products slowly started to become established throughout the country. As Don Randall recalls: 'It's hard to say who had the greatest influence on the sales. Arthur Smith was a big influence at one time, and other people had a part in it, but I don't think there was anybody who made us say "Boy, they are selling a lot of guitars for us." People would say, "You must sell a lot of those guitars down in Texas or Oklahoma" but that wasn't true – we sold guitars and amplifiers wherever there were people. It didn't make any difference where it was, if it was Oklahoma or Texas or Florida – the second largest country music area in the United States at that time was around Boston!'

At the time of the Telecaster's introduction the company was kept afloat by the income brought in by Leo's wife, who worked for a local telephone company. Leo's vision must have seemed hopelessly idealistic in these uncertain days before the Telecaster became established. By 1951, however, the guitar had made it, and Fender amplifiers had gained an even wider clientele. Even so, Leo's concerns were still centered on engineering excellence rather than profit. Don Randall: 'Leo had a strange sense of humor. We'd go to lunch at times and he'd see a new car outside by the curb. He'd get down on his back in the street, and crawl under the car to see how it was built and say, "Can you imagine them building a car this way;

they don't have [this] or they don't have [that]!" And we'd be saying "Leo, get up off the street, for crying out loud"!'

This obsession with improving or redefining old-fashioned designs would pay dividends as Leo moved on to his next project.

BASS MOTIVES

Although the Fender Telecaster was a crystalization of ideas that were being simultaneously explored by several different designers, Leo's next creation, the Precision Bass, was inspiringly original: a completely new instrument that would significantly change the sound of popular music.

On his visits to working musicians, Leo had taken note of the problems encountered by bass players, who at that time had to use upright string basses which were hard to play, difficult to transport, and notoriously tricky to amplify. By applying the technology of the Telecaster to the string bass, Leo liberated the bassist from what he called the 'doghouse'; later he would point out that his new instrument allowed the bassist to join in synchronized dancing, too!

The Precision Bass, released in 1951, was a revolutionary reworking of the old-fashioned upright bass. Leo flipped it on its side and gave it a radically shaped solid body and a fretted guitar-style neck. The latter feature allowed guitar players doubling on bass to pitch notes perfectly. The genius of Leo's design is perhaps best illustrated by the fact that every one of the main design features of the Precision is carried over into modern basses: the twin cutaways, the scale length, the large tuners. Even on this very first example of the bass guitar, Leo anticipated all of the major problems of comfort and playability, by adding an upper 'horn' to improve balance. Although the body would later lose its Tele-style hard edges, Leo's shape for the bass is still the standard for modern bass guitars; in fact, for the first few years of the instrument's life the term 'Fender bass' assumed a generic status, like Hoover or Band-Aid. By the end of the decade, the electric bass would almost completely supplant its cumbersome predecessor.

Although both the Telecaster and the Precision Bass were radically new instruments, both gained acceptance within a surprisingly short time. The Telecaster wasn't a rock 'n' roll instrument but a cowboy's guitar, its creamy finish and black pickguard perfectly matching the average C&W singer's outfit. Notwithstanding, it found its way on to blues records remarkably quickly: B.B. King recalls buying one of the first Esquires (the single-pickup version of the Tele), while the likes of James Burton would soon introduce the instrument in the rockabilly field. The Precision started to win a following in Leo's favored country genre, but by the mid Fifties was becoming a fixture on both rock and blues records. Perhaps the most obvious symptom of Fender's success was the reaction of its competitors. Gibson started work on its own solid body electric in 1951, which came to be known as the Les Paul, and launched its unsuccessful violin-shaped EB electric bass guitar in 1953; Gretsch would launch its own solid (though heavily routed under the top) line in 1954, while manufacturers such as Harmony, Kay and Silvertone would soon follow suit.

Fender's audacious rise had caught everyone by surprise. In addition to the Telecaster, Fender could now boast a line of amplifiers which were well on their way to becoming the premier brand in the US. More surprising still was the ambition of Leo Fender, Don Randall and the rest of the company to play with the big boys. To match Gibson at its own game they needed a more extended guitar line, and in particular an up-market model that would keep the company's technological lead over its competitors. Their next model would fulfill that role to perfection.

The Precision Bass: Leo's radical masterstroke

19

A CLASSIC IS BORN

The Stratocaster was a masterstroke in electric guitar design – yet it was conceived as simply an

upmarket complement to the Telecaster. The foresight of Leo Fender and his team would

produce a radical instrument that would still seem contemporary forty years on.

BEYOND THE CANOE PADDLE

By the beginning of 1953 Leo Fender's company was starting to be taken seriously. Granted, they still had to put up with jibes about producing guitars that looked like breadboards or toilet seats, but Fender steel guitars, Fender amplifiers and the revolutionary Telecaster had won many fans in the country music field. The company was expanding rapidly, moving into new premises and fine-tuning its sales and distribution arrangements.

All the company's major figures were intent on making the company a major player in the guitar field, and for that they needed an upmarket, more luxurious model that would compete with the well-crafted guitars from Gibson, Gretsch, Epiphone and others.

The marketing-led motives behind the production of Fender's new model would result in a model that was radically different from its predecessors, the Telecaster and the Precision Bass. Both

Bill Carson outside the Broken Spoke Club, Austin, Texas

of these workmanlike, utilitarian instruments had been launched purely as a result of Leo Fender's vision – at the time of their introduction there was certainly no established market for a solid body electric guitar or bass. However, by 1953 companies like Gibson had jumped on the solid electric bandwagon with its Les Paul Model and the Fender company was determined to keep ahead.

According to Don Randall, who started distributing Fender products after the War and later became head of sales of the newly established sales division, the initial aims for the new guitar were quite clear: 'The decision to introduce a new guitar mainly came from the sales department. The principal need was to have something to fill a market slot with – to have a better-looking product, which looked more sophisticated than the Telecaster.'

It was Don Randall who had to put up with the most jibes about the Telecaster from jealous rivals and bemused dealers: 'I got all kinds of snide remarks, like "What do you do, paddle your canoe with that thing?", or "They'd make good snow shovels!" We were competing with Gibson, who had 80 years of experience over us, and they had guitars with bound fingerboards and fancy finishes, so we felt the need to upgrade and provide something that gave them a little competition in that field. And when you more or less saturate the market with something like the Telecaster, naturally you move into a more expensive product. It was much like the motor companies having five or six differently priced models.'

Although the Stratocaster was to provide the Fender equivalent to Ford's upmarket Lincoln and Mercury brands, Leo Fender and his team were not interested in merely adding a few chrome embellishments to the existing model. The Stratocaster would be designed from the ground up. Work began in earnest around the time the company moved to new premises on Pomona Street, Fullerton early in 1953. Around this time Leo Fender recruited some of his main collaborators. Although there was no doubt that the overall

Freddie Tavares (second from left) discusses guitar design with Leo Fender (center) and Clint Walker (second from right)

vision for what would become the Stratocaster belonged to Leo himself, these collaborators would have an important influence on the final form the guitar would take. After all, Leo, who'd taken a few piano and saxophone lessons in his youth, was no guitarist.

THE FACES BEHIND THE STRATOCASTER

Leo's closest assistant throughout the work on what would become the Stratocaster was Freddie Tavares. Freddie was of Hawaiian extraction, and had played with several outfits, including Harry Owens and the Royal Hawaiians; he is also to be heard playing pedal steel guitar on the *Loony Toons* theme. Most Fender employees of the time seem to echo Don Randall's description of him: 'Freddie was a delightful, delightful man. He had a great sense of humor, he was very intelligent, and an excellent musician.' Tavares was also an accomplished draftsman, and although Leo Fender had been experimenting with different pickup designs ever since the launch of the Precision Bass, it was not until Tavares joined that work on the new guitar started in earnest.

Leo Fender liked to surround himself with a community of musicians, and could often be found in the local clubs with guitarists who were field-testing his equipment. One such figure was

Bill Carson, a Western Swing guitarist who would play a key role in the development of the new instrument. Carson had approached Leo around 1951 to buy an electric guitar: 'He let me have one, I think it was a Telecaster or a Broadcaster together with an amp, for eighteen bucks a month. Soon after that we became friends, and it was after that that I started telling him what was wrong with his damn old Telecaster.'

Western Swing musician Bill Carson, featured here in a Fifties Fender ad

Together, Leo Fender, Freddie Tavares, Bill Carson and the sales team came up with a blueprint for the new guitar. It was obvious that they needed a new body shape, while all parties were keen on including a vibrato unit. According to Forrest White, who took charge of production in 1954: 'It was around that time that Paul Bigsby had come out with his vibrato, or tremolo, whatever you want to call it. People seemed to like the sound real well, so we thought the Stratocaster should have one too.'

HORNS OF PLENTY
Although the Stratocaster's 'twin horn' design was revolutionary, the basic shape was in fact derived from Leo's earlier Precision Bass. Early Precision prototypes featured a Telecaster-derived shape, but the extra neck length and large headstock made it neck-heavy, so that it was uncomfortable to play and wouldn't balance when played standing up with a strap. Extending the upper bout, producing an upper 'horn', was the simplest way of improving the instrument's balance. This, of course, made the Precision into what is now termed a 'double cutaway' instrument, although this description is to some extent

misleading, as the body shape actually gained a horn, rather than having some of its wood removed.

But while the body shape of the Stratocaster was derived from that of the Precision, it was a far more elegant creation. The basic slab shape, two-horn design of the Precision was transformed into a sculpted shape that Fender would later term the 'Custom Contour' body. Forrest White vividly recalls where the inspiration for the body shape came from: 'There were two guys who helped influence how the body was made, and they were Rex Galleon and Bill Carson. I remember Bill said to Leo, "this guitar should fit you like a shirt." Now when Bill was talking about shirts he meant the Western kind of shirt, and those babies fit tight! So what he meant was that he wanted an instrument that was going to be snug, and that was comfortable to play.'

Carson remembers the Telecaster's slab shape as being one of its biggest drawbacks:

'The body was too square, it dug into my rib. So what I wanted was something that had what I called body reliefs – later on I think George Fullerton's wife put the word "Contour" to it. Now people often talk about the body just in terms of the visuals, but the important thing was that when you pick that guitar up, it's like shaking hands with an old friend. Your arm wasn't stuck in the "cocked" position as it was with the Telecaster or the big old jazz-bodied guitars.'

Leo Fender and Freddie Tavares responded to Galleon and Carson's suggestions by sculpting away the back of the body and contouring the front; the result was a shape which was an aesthetic and ergonomic masterpiece. For the first time in the electric guitar's history it had gained a shape of its own, as opposed to one inherited from its arch-top cousins.

There were many more elements that went to make up the final recipe of the Stratocaster. Bill Carson recollects: 'I wanted the vibrato because with the vibrato to play pedal steel glisses, and a tone and volume foot pedal, I could sometimes get

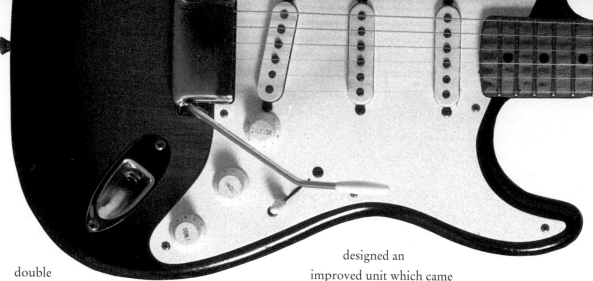

The Stratocaster 'tremolo' unit set a new design standard, which has since been much copied

double scale on recording sessions. And I wanted the six bridges to intonate, so it would play in tune and you could play with brass sections and the like. I wanted four or five pickups for the differences in tones. And I wanted the big headstock like Paul Bigsby had on his guitar.' Although Carson's claim to have contributed '95 percent of the ideas that made up the Stratocaster' at first glance appears inconsistent with statements by Forrest White and others, that 'the Stratocaster wasn't designed for any one person,' there's no doubt that input from musicians was vital in shaping the Strat – and Carson was the main musical consultant. But as George Fullerton put it, 'The final version of the guitar was the result of all the different things we tried – it was a trial and error kind of thing. The only thing I know is that eventually the shape was the one that Leo himself decided was the way to go, regardless of who had the initial idea, 'cause Leo always had the last word in design. An idea had to be proven to be a positive idea before he even considered it.'

TREM LINES

The Stratocaster 'tremolo' was a vital element in the guitar's success. It's worth pointing out, however, that the unit should really be termed a 'vibrato' unit, as the term tremolo refers to a change in volume rather than in pitch. Fender could be justified in making the mistake because vibrato units were still a comparative novelty when the Strat was developed. The first units had appeared on Rickenbacker guitars, but Paul Bigsby had designed an improved unit which came onto the market around 1950, and was soon available as an optional extra on Gibson and Gretsch guitars. The Bigsby vibrato worked by wrapping the end of the guitar strings around a steel rod, which rotated as the vibrato arm was waggled, stretching the strings and varying the pitch. It was a more effective unit than anything else on the market, but had to be used very carefully if the guitar was not to go out of tune. When Leo Fender and Freddie Tavares set out to produce their own version they aimed to do better, and minimize the tuning problems.

Leo Fender, the man who liked looking under cars to check out their suspension, was in his element when working on this engineering problem, and many observers commented that the Strat tremolo was 'Leo's pride and joy'. However, it was also the source of an early disaster. Leo's initial design was rather like a Bigsby unit, with a tailpiece which could be moved by the tremolo arm, and a bridge which used roller saddles to reduce friction and improve tuning stability. The comparatively lightweight tailpiece and the bridge saddles soaked up the string vibrations and damaged the sustain. Bill Carson: 'I took this guitar to a job, hooked it up to play it, and it sounded like a cheap banjo, the sound decayed so quick. So I phoned Leo and Freddie up and said: "You guys wrecked my guitar, the pickups are no good any more." And they said "We didn't do anything to the pickups!" And that was when we found that the mass of the tremolo bar can boost the sustain of the guitar.'

By this time, around the end of 1953, the

company had already tooled up to produce the guitar with the faulty vibrato unit. Leo and Freddie spent many hours wrestling with the problem and trying to restore the guitar's natural sustain, but in the end were forced to give up and start the design again from scratch. The expensive tooling was scrapped. Twenty years later Leo Fender would still recall the problem and the scrapping of $5000 worth of tooling with a wince.

Once they'd been forced to start over, Leo and Freddie came up with a far more original design within a couple of months. The second unit was unlike anything that had gone before: it was what is now termed a 'fulcrum unit' which pivoted around six screws. Both bridge and tailpiece were now in one unit, which pivoted at the front, and were balanced against the string tension by means of five adjustable springs underneath the body. The top unit consisted of a chromed plate and six adjustable bridge saddles; the strings passed through six holes in this plate and were anchored via a heavy milled steel inertia bar. This solid construction retained the guitar's natural sustain, and by minimizing the travel of the strings over the bridge saddles offered improved tuning without the need for the roller saddles which had helped to ruin the guitar's sustain. Unlike the Bigsby equivalent, the unit offered room for adjustment; the guitarist could remove one or more of the springs and alter their tension, allowing the use of

the unit with different gauge strings.

The design features of the Stratocaster Synchronized Tremolo didn't stop there. Its predecessor, the Telecaster, had featured three simple bridge saddles, which allowed the intonation to be adjusted for each pair of strings. At the time the facility for any form of intonation adjustment was almost unheard-of; most electric guitars had simple wooden bridges on which there was little facility for alteration. Movable saddles, like those of the Telecaster, allowed the guitarist to adjust the setup for different string heights or weights, and ensure that the fretted notes played perfectly in tune. This facility was groundbreaking for a production instrument – at the time only one other company, Melita, offered anything better, with a bridge that was available on Gretsch guitars from 1951. But while the Telecaster's bridge might have offered unprecedented potential for adjustment, for Bill Carson the arrangement was a long way short of satisfactory: 'You couldn't tune it then, and you can't tune it now if it's got three bridges on it. So I sawed my bridges in two so you could intonate it properly. You couldn't do that properly without six bridges, 'cause it was a physical impossibility.'

Thanks to Carson's suggestions, the new unit featured six separate bridge saddles, each made of pressed steel, with two screws to adjust the height of each saddle, and an intonation screw which, according to Carson, was at the front of the bridge

1954 patent document illustrates principles behind Fender's 'synchronized tremolo unit'

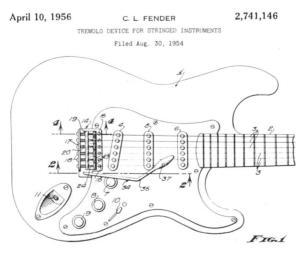

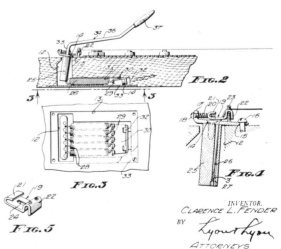

April 10, 1956   C. L. FENDER   2,741,146

TREMOLO DEVICE FOR STRINGED INSTRUMENTS

Filed Aug. 30, 1954

on early designs: 'Originally the bridge adjusted from the back side, the back side being where the pickups are. And I broke a string with that configuration, and it was almost impossible to intonate. So the next day Leo and Freddie turned the whole thing around a hundred and eighty degrees, and put it in the position that you see on Stratocasters now.' With six separate saddles, the bridge offered excellent control of intonation, bettering most of the guitar's rivals, while the individual height adjustment for each string was an unqualified first. Crucially, thanks to extensive field testing, the complex assembly also sounded good. Leo Fender spent much time working with his tooling company, Race & Olmsted, on a bridge saddle design which offered the necessary adjustment without incurring unwanted movement or vibration, while the solid inertia block and even the vibrato springs both contributed to the guitar's clear and sustained sound.

The Stratocaster's neck stayed fairly close to the design of its predecessor. Like the Tele, it was made from a single piece of maple with the truss rod installed from the back and the necessary routing concealed by a 'skunk stripe' of walnut. The truss rod, and thus the relief or 'bow' of the neck, could be adjusted via a screw at the base of the neck. Although this point was rather more difficult to get to, requiring the removal of the pickguard, it made the neck far less prone to breakage than its rivals. The method of installing frets was also unique: Leo designed a machine to cut the fret slots automatically, which he claimed gave more accurate results than any of the opposition, while the frets themselves were inserted directly into the neck rather than via a separate fingerboard. Although Leo probably selected the maple of the neck primarily for aesthetic reasons, he chose a one-piece construction so that when a string was fretted its vibration would pass directly into the neck, thus improving sustain. Few other makers, before or since, were as obsessed with retaining the structural integrity of a guitar as was Leo.

The main difference between a Strat neck and a

Billy Gray and His Western Swing Band use *Fender* Fine Electric Instruments
The Nation's No. 1 New Big Western Band Exclusively

Billy Gray and his Fender-equipped Western Swing band. Bill Carson poses with his Stratocaster in the center

Tele neck is, of course, the headstock. The Strat's headstock shape was perhaps the one source of controversy about the new design, because it bore a distinct resemblance to the headstock of Paul Bigsby's guitars made for Merle Travis. Leo himself said in 1978 that 'the shape came from wanting to preserve straight string pull – it goes back to instruments from Croatia'. Bill Carson, on the other hand, says that he urged Leo to copy the shape of Bigsby's designs, saying that 'that skinny headstock of the Telecaster has no beauty in it; it looks like a pretty girl with bad clothes on. Paul Bigsby had built a big headstock guitar for Merle Travis, and I wanted that particular head stuck on my guitar'. Leo Fender had definitely seen some of Paul Bigsby's guitars, and must have been aware of the similarity of his headstock. It seems likely that he recognized its elegance and engineering efficiency, and decided to use a similar design, not realizing the significance that posterity would assign to its shape. In any case, the headstock design was an efficient one: placing the tuners along one side made them easier to use, while the 'straight string pull' of the design meant the strings didn't kink or splay out as they went over the nut. This minimized any hitching at the nut when bending strings or using the tremolo, and helped the guitar's general tuning stability.

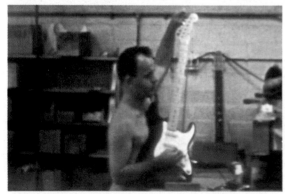

Although the Strat was ideal for mass production, these factory shots show how much of it was hand-made

Fender designs were also unique in that the headstock did not 'tilt back' – its face was parallel to the neck itself. Reckoned by many makers to be an integral part of the Fender sound, this design also made the headstock less prone to breakage, helping to make the Strat one of the sturdiest guitar designs ever. Ironically, although the headstock was the only part of the Stratocaster that resembled another guitar, that same element is now seen as one of the most unique Fender hallmarks. Other manufacturers have since copied Stratocaster designs, but they have been forced to use other headstock shapes to avoid lawsuits from Fender.

THREE'S A CROWD

Right from the beginning of the design process, it was obvious that the Stratocaster would have three pickups. Like many of the guitar's other features, this decision was marketing-led, and gave Don Randall's salesmen an extra feature to tout. As Forrest White recalls, 'Leo said to me "I got to thinking, if two pickups are better than one, why not have three?" So we decided to go for three pickups.' Working on the principle of 'the more the merrier', Bill Carson asked Leo to give the new instrument four pickups instead. Carson recalls Leo telling him that 'there wasn't enough room to have four pickups, so I wound up with three – I didn't get as many as I wanted'. In fact three pickups gave a more useful choice of tones than four; and although the Fender Company would subsequently experiment with four pickup guitars it would never introduce them commercially.

Even before the Strat had officially reached the drawing board, Leo Fender had been experimenting with new pickup designs. Right through the development process he put meticulous work into voicing the pickups, testing different gauge wire and different polepiece heights, all of which gave different tonal balances, until the final staggered polepiece version was designed. Each of the three pickups was of identical design, but the bridge pickup was distinctively angled; this position kept the treble 'twang' without sacrificing the bottom end of the bass strings.

The Strat's distinctive three-way pickup switch – which guitarists later discovered could be lodged in 'in-between' positions – has become a standard for pickup switches, and has been frequently copied. In fact, the original was simply a unit readily available from Leo Fender's radio industry suppliers. It did the job, which as far as Leo was concerned was all that mattered.

When it came to fixing the pickups in position, Leo once again defied convention by mounting all the electronics on a single ply plastic pickguard. By this method the guitar's body only required simple routing, while the wiring could be performed away from the guitar – a boon for mass production, which also simplified repair and replacement. The output socket was also unusual, being mounted on a snazzy chrome plate, an idea apparently suggested by George Fullerton to prevent the guitarist having to search around when wanting to plug in.

MORE THAN THE SUM OF ITS PARTS

Taken individually, it's fairly easy to understand why each element of the Stratocaster turned out the way it did. The Stratocaster was essentially a straightforward engineering solution to a number of different problems. However, the history of the electric guitar has shown that few makers understood these engineering solutions adequately. The Strat was more than a collection of diverse elements – more than the sum of its parts, it added up to an inspiring whole that in practical terms was way ahead of the competition.

Ironically, it was Leo Fender's lack of knowledge of traditional guitar production that helped make the instrument so effective – rather than rely on traditional solutions, he tackled each problem from scratch. Each element of the Stratocaster was the result of empirical testing, and although the company was keen to give the instrument new features or gimmicks to help sell it, the extensive field testing meant that each of those gimmicks was, in fact, a genuinely useful feature. According to the recollections of Fender employees, the final work on the instrument was completed remarkably quickly following the initial tremolo debacle, with the model ready for production around May 1954. The final requirement for this impressive package was a name; this came from Don Randall, who had also christened the Telecaster:

'When we came up with a name for the first guitar it was brand new, and so was broadcasting, so I figured the Broadcaster would be a good name for it. Then when the Fred Gretsch company told us they used that name for their drums it was necessary to go to another title, so I figured the next name after broadcasting was television, hence Telecaster. Then when we got another guitar going, people were talking about going to the moon and shooting rockets off or whatever, and that involved the stratosphere, so we came up with Stratocaster.'

Fender's publicity material to launch this new instrument points out its advantages. It seems, in retrospect, somewhat restrained, sticking to elu-

cidating specific design elements rather than indulging in hyperbole. It stressed the advantages of the tremolo unit 'which provides easy action and a full tone pitch change, both above and below the basic tuning, plus the fact that the guitar will remain in tune even after long playing'. Fender reckoned that the body design was 'probably the most comfortable instrument to play ever to be made' – and they were probably right. The literature also pointed out the capacity for adjustment of string height and intonation, the guitar's natural sustain and other features such as the handy output jack. At a time when most other manufacturers were offering gimmicks, every one of the Stratocaster's features was a genuine innovation. In fact, so advanced was the guitar, it would take guitarists over a decade to catch up with it and appreciate its qualitiesß.

This early Strat is probably an early employee one-off, and boasts a padded pickguard

Eldon Shamblin (right) holds the gold metallic Strat given to him by Leo Fender early in the model's history. Bill Carson holds one of its successors

CHAPTER THREE

WHY THE STRAT SUCCEEDED

It was more than good looks that turned the Stratocaster into an icon. In practical terms Leo Fender's invention far surpassed its rivals, which were rendered outdated overnight. From its bridge through to its headstock, each element was finely considered.

Forty years after its launch the Strat has retained its glamor despite its relative familiarity. Even so, it's hard to imagine just how revolutionary it must have seemed at the time of its launch in 1954. Those who were there, such as Hank Marvin, remember that 'it was a little bit like seeing an instrument from another planet; it just didn't look like a guitar'. That was entirely true, for every other guitar on the market at the time featured a shape derived from old-fashioned archtop models. Yet the Strat's ergonomics more than matched its looks, and opened up a massive technology gap between Fender and its competitors.

When launched in 1954, the Strat was the nearest thing to a perfect guitar design as could be imagined. There was nothing to which it could be compared. Even the Strat's best-known rival, the Gibson Les Paul, launched in 1952 as a response to the Telecaster, was a shadow of the legend it would later become. The Les Paul Model, available in May 1954, possessed a rudimentary bridge design which was clumsy with little potential for adjustment. It would take Gibson until 1958 to produce the classic Les Paul Standard Model. Other manufacturers did little better. Rickenbacker had some innovative guitars, but would never attain the classic simplicity of the Strat, while Gretsch guitars were sexy but comparatively

impractical. The remainder of the competition trailed even further behind. Gibson, Rickenbacker and Gretsch are still making fine guitars, many of which are close relatives of their early Fifties models, but none of these has remained as true to its initial design concept as the Strat. Fender's current line of Stratocasters incorporates several models with updated features, but the original vintage-style Strat, as released in 1954, is still one of the company's most popular models.

BETWEEN THE BUTTONS

The Strat might have looked futuristic, but it wouldn't have become an icon if it hadn't sounded

The Strat's pickup switch officially gave three different sounds – guitarists soon discovered five

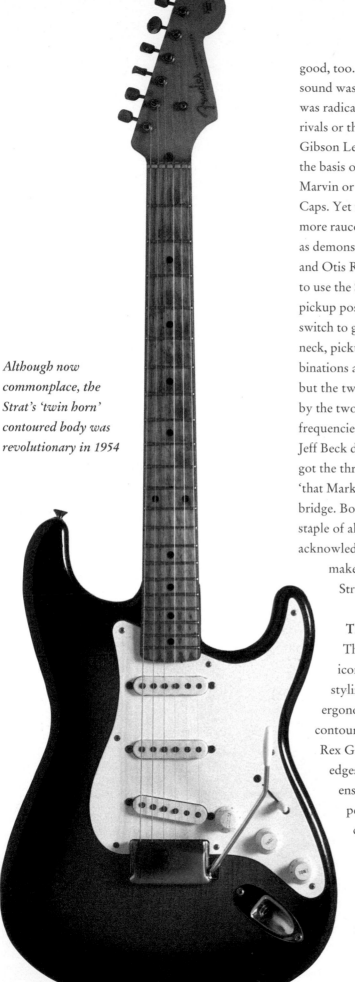

Although now commonplace, the Strat's 'twin horn' contoured body was revolutionary in 1954

good, too. At the time of the Strat's launch, its sound was unique: the clean, clear, sustained tone was radically different from that of its archtop rivals or the comparatively mellow-sounding Gibson Les Paul. It was this sound which formed the basis of records by Buddy Holly, Hank Marvin or Johnny Meeks of Gene Vincent's Blue Caps. Yet the Strat was also suitable for a different, more raucous sound with a cranked up amplifier, as demonstrated by players such as Buddy Guy and Otis Rush. These players were among the first to use the Strat's 'in-between' or 'out-of-phase' pickup positions, lodging the three-way pickup switch to give middle and bridge, or middle and neck, pickups simultaneously. These pickup combinations are not, in electronic terms, out of phase, but the two slightly different signals produced by the two pickups interact, canceling out some frequencies and emphasizing others to give what Jeff Beck describes as 'a needly sound, but it's still got the throat there' for middle and neck, and 'that Mark Knopfler sound' for middle and bridge. Both these sounds have since become a staple of almost every Strat player, a fact Fender acknowledged by fitting five-way switches, which make in-between selection easier, to the Strat from 1977.

THE SHAPE OF THINGS TO COME

The Strat's streamlined body is a modern icon evocative of the classic automobile styling of the Fifties. This design has ergonomic as well as aesthetic pluses. The contoured body, suggested by Bill Carson and Rex Galleon, was comfortable with no sharp edges, and the characteristic twin horns ensured an even balance. More importantly perhaps, the horns introduced the concept of twin cutaways – paring down the guitar's body to enable greater physical communion between player and instrument. The influence of this concept was so profound that some manufacturers offered barely concealed interpretations of the Strat shape, while others simply adapted the twin cutaway idea to their own needs.

The form of the Strat's body also had real sonic advantages. Freddie Tavares summed up the concept of the body design when he told Dick Dale: 'If you could put strings across a telegraph pole, you'd have the purest, sweetest sounds in the world. But you can't pick up a telegraph pole.' The Strat's body, lusciously contoured but reassuringly solid, is an ergonomic version of a telegraph pole.

TECHNICAL TRICKS

The Strat featured technical advances almost literally from head to tail. The Strat's headstock was designed to retain 'straight string pull' – the strings pass over the nut in a straight line. The Strat's maple neck was an integral part of the guitar's sound – later guitars with rosewood fingerboards would sound slightly mellow in comparison. Some guitarists, such as Eric Clapton, prefer the bite of a maple neck, others such as Rory Gallagher opt for the relative warmth of the later version.

The Strat's tremolo was a functional masterpiece for its time. Experience has also shown that it makes its own contribution to the instrument's sound – players such as David Gilmour believe that the pressed steel saddles of early guitars sound distinctly different from later cast versions. Although the tremolo was designed for fairly conservative use, the likes of Jimi Hendrix and Eddie Van Halen went to extremes, forging a

'Straight string pull' design means strings pass in straight lines to machine heads, reducing friction and consequent tuning problems

new guitar style in the process. Modern tremolo designs, such as that on the American Standard Strat or Paul Reed Smith's influential Custom guitar, eliminate some of the sources of friction found in the original Strat design, but still remain faithful to the basic concept.

SAFETY IN NUMBERS

Many observers have described Leo Fender as the Henry Ford of the electric guitar because his designs were perfect for mass production. Fender instruments could be made by employees with little experience of traditional musical instrument manufacture, while the whole construction of the guitar was ideal for modular assembly. Bodies were simple to rout, while all the wiring could be performed away from the guitar, and fitted late in the production process.

Although Fender products were certainly ideal for mass production, the Fender factory in the Fifties was not highly automated – only a few processes, such as cutting the slots for frets, were performed by dedicated machines. But the ease with which the Strat could be produced would become a major factor in its success – ironically, it was also a major factor in the success of its imitators. Despite the odium now attached to Fender guitars of the Seventies, the CBS-owned Fender company was paradoxically extremely successful, selling immense numbers of guitars in a decade when many other American manufacturers went out of business.

THE ROLE OF LUCK

When analyzing the process by which Leo Fender designed the Strat, it's obvious that by starting from basic principles he came up with a truly effective design. Yet the true mark of his genius – and maybe luck – is how features of the guitar would only become apparent after its launch. First, the 'in-between' pickup selections, a vital part of the guitar's sound which Leo hadn't envisioned. Yet, as others have shown, if Leo hadn't placed the pickups correctly, or had attempted to fit four pickups, this 'in-between' sound wouldn't have worked. Factors such as the weight and the choice of woods seem to be magically right in a way that has become obvious as Fender and other makers have tinkered with the basic design. As John Page of the Fender Custom Shop puts it: 'From talking to Leo, I think he was an everyday guy who wanted to make everyday guitars for everyday players. Some of it was genius and some of it was luck . . . It was a magical combination.'

1955 Stratocaster. In most respects it is identical to current models

CHAPTER FOUR

THE FENDER YEARS

Leo Fender's radical guitar and amplifier designs would come to form the basis of one of

America's biggest musical instrument manufacturers. But in subsequent years the company

would endure radical changes in fortune and, by the Eighties, threats of imminent closure.

Although Leo Fender had started out to improve the lot of the country musician specifically, his inventions had a much wider impact and were responsible for creating a whole new generation of musicians. Leo's Stratocaster was ushered into the market in 1954, the year generally credited as the birth date of rock 'n' roll.

Electric music had been growing in popularity ever since the Second World War, and by 1954 the inclusion of an electric guitar in a pop band's line-up was standard. This coincided with a general trend away from the big bands of the prewar era, in favor of more compact – and louder – electrified units. Not all, nor even a majority, of the electric guitars in use were Fenders, for Gibson's old-fashioned electrified archtops were still the choice of most R&B or country musicians. If anything, it was Fender amplifiers which established

the company's early reputation. These powerful and reliable workhorses offered twin speaker configurations well before most of the competition. By 1952 the line consisted of six models, ranging from the topline Twin and Bassman, down to the small Princeton; the Twin and Bassman, in particular, would become standard for tube guitar amps, and even subsequent amps like the English Marshall line would be based on Fender circuitry. The advent of the Stratocaster helped confirm Fender's technical lead over the competition. After a steady start, sales would gradually increase over the next decade.

TOOLING UP FOR A MUSIC REVOLUTION

In late 1953 the Fender company relocated to a much larger new site at South Raymond Avenue in Fullerton to cope with an increase in demand for its products. Before this move the pressures on Fender staff were immense; George Fullerton remembers Fender employees occasionally sanding or finishing products outside the old building because of the shortage of space. Fender products were, in general, ideal for mass production, but in the early days production methods were somewhat haphazard – one good example is that employees were not allocated specific tasks. In May 1954, industrial engineer Forrest White was brought in to organize the production system. White quickly discovered that Fender's employees were largely well-motivated and turned out an

Fender's Research and Development building in the early Sixties

impressive product – and that Leo would be his biggest problem.

'A lot of these people who write about the history of Fender, if only they knew that, especially on our professional amplifiers, there were hardly two runs that went out that were the same. If we finished a production run in January, say, then made another one in June for the same model, there'd be changes because Leo Fender was never satisfied with what he was giving the musician at a particular time. All that was going through his mind was "How can I make it better?" He had it in mind that the product he built would be second to none, and I think he proved his point.'

Controlling Leo Fender's tendency to alter components without informing anyone became White's major bugbear, and made proper stock control and testing almost impossible goals. As the Fender Musical Instrument Company expanded, so the organization of production processes had to be made to improve radically. Under White's direction, with incentive schemes for Fender employees, the company began to achieve consistent production of instruments that are now regarded as classics. According to Randall, 'Forrest had to overcome a lot of obstacles and put up with a lot that he shouldn't have had to put

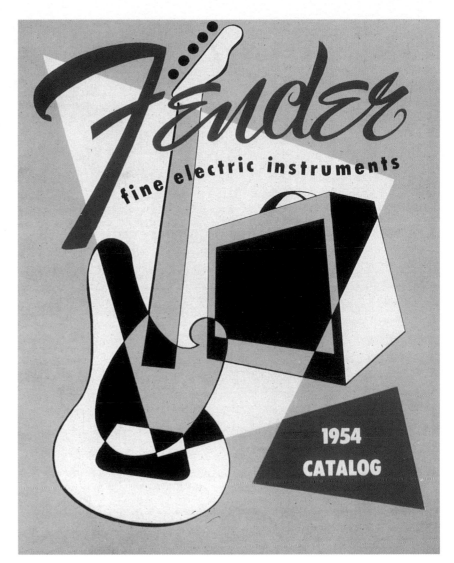

1954 Fender catalogue embodies Fifties' design trends

up with, but he took a bad situation and made it run very efficiently.'

An improvement in mass production was vital if Fender was to remain at the heart of the musical revolution now underway. Between 1955 and 1960 the market for electric guitars expanded enormously, as a new generation took to the instrument. Fender solids had become popular with many Chicago blues players, with several guitarists citing Earl Hooker as an influential Stratocaster player. By 1960 both Buddy Guy and Otis Rush were established as Strat users, while Buddy Holly was the single most important Strat user among rock artists. Don Randall: 'In those early days we weren't really conscious of who was playing our instruments in the rock 'n' roll field – we weren't too close to the situation, and I don't

Cutting a guitar neck outside the Pomona factory

*Fender boasted huge
numbers of unofficial
endorsees in the Fifties:
Gene Vincent was one
of the official ones*

think we were sophisticated enough at the time to know what to do in a case like that.' Nonetheless, the unofficial endorsees helped generate a growth in Fender sales, which also extended beyond the USA. 'We exported more musical equipment than all the rest of the music manufacturers combined at one time,' recalls Randall. 'A lot of the business stemmed from the GIs stationed overseas, principally in Germany, who would buy these things, then they'd be playing in the local clubs and the locals would see them and want them.'

FOLLOWING A CLASS ACT

Fender did not remain idle after the launch of the Strat. Two of the company's most popular models were launched in 1956: the budget model Musicmaster, with a single pickup, and a two-pickup version, the DuoSonic. Both utilized a twin-horn body similar to that of the Strat, but were made with a shorter scale to enhance their suitability for novices. Simple hardware and the

absence of body contouring reduced costs to make them Fender's cheapest electrics, at $149 for the Duo-Sonic and $119 for the single-pickup version. Two years later the company augmented the guitar line with the Jazzmaster, which furthered the contour-body idea by featuring an 'offset waist' design to allow a more comfortable playing position. This model also featured a new, sophisticated tremolo unit, which offered a lighter feel and could be locked to avoid detuning in the event of string breakage. Its large pickups were intended to give it a mellower tone than the Strat or Tele, and the Jazzmaster soon caught on with America's newly emerging surf groups, rather than its intended jazz market. However, neither the Jazzmaster nor 1962's Jaguar, a similar but shorter-scale model with different pickups and switching, would enjoy the longevity of the Strat.

Ergonomic improvements were not the only advances the company introduced in the late Fifties; in 1957, to vie with flash multicolored

*Fender Custom Colors,
such as the Candy
Apple Red of this
Strat, became an offi-
cial factory option
around 1957*

models from Gretsch and other makers, Fender introduced its famous custom finishes. Up to this point Fender had made one-off guitars in non-standard finishes for favored musicians who dealt direct with the factory. Now George Fullerton had the idea of introducing a standard range of brightly colored finishes: 'I had the idea of intro-ducing a new color that was different from any-thing we'd done before, and went over to a local paint shop to get them to mix up this color. When I had a Jazzmaster prototype sprayed up in the red I'd had mixed the whole sales force laughed at the idea, but it soon became successful, particularly in Europe.' Custom Colors were officially introduced in late 1956, for a five percent price premium. Since then the comparative rarity of Custom Color Fenders from the Fifties and early

Sonic Blue Strat: Fender finishes echoed popular automobile finishes of the time

Sixties has made them particular favorites with vintage guitar buffs, and they are now worth far more than their standard-finish brethren.

YOU WON'T PART WITH YOURS EITHER

By the late Fifties Fender had shaken many of its competitors to the core. Ted McCarty, who at the time was general manager of Fender's arch rivals Gibson, remembers constant criticism from dealers who complained that 'Gibson never came up with new ideas'. There was a distinct culture gap between the California revolutionaries and the Kalamazoo establishment as represented by Gibson. An effective press campaign by Fender would underline the company's new-fangled image. A series of advertisements showed Fender users in a collection of bizarre situations – surfing, skydiving from a plane or climbing a telegraph pole – with the slogan, 'You Won't Part With Yours Either'.

'Everything in the music business at that time was pretty stereotyped,' reckons Don Randall. 'We wanted something to kind of jar people loose. So we had a lot of things: the guy walking into the surf with his flippers on, the kid in the barber's chair. We had a really cute one of a kid walking down a dusty lane pulling a guitar and an amplifier on a little wagon. The dust was rising up and he had a little straw hat on, and it looked like a halo around his head – it was a heck of a deal. Then there's the one with the sky-diver, and it's the greatest photo I ever saw – you can see the desert floor way below him and everything. It was a very effective campaign, and we got letters about it from all over.'

By 1964 the British invasion increased the interest in the electric guitar to an almost feverish extent. Even though the Beatles didn't at first use Fender – despite Don Randall's attempts to persuade Brian Epstein to have them endorse Fender products – the growth in rock music saw guitar production rise through the roof, to the point where Fender was making 1500 guitars a week, 30 times the number it was making a decade earlier. The company was back-ordered on many of its lines; Leo Fender later quoted a figure of 150,000 for the Mustang guitar alone. Fender was a victim of its own success, and faced the threat of creating

You won't part with yours either*

Wherever you go, you'll find Fender

Fender's 'You Won't Part With Yours Either' campaign emphasized the company's lively and original approach

a market for electric guitars which it could not satisfy, thereby allowing the competition a foot in the door. But the steps which would be taken to help the company expand to satisfy this market would later be regarded as disastrous by many of Fender's musician customers.

THE CBS YEARS

If there's one term that adds to the value of an old Strat, it's pre-CBS. The Columbia Broadcasting System company bought Fender in January 1965, and for many guitarists that point was seen to be one at which the quality of Fender instruments declined. Whatever its eventual results, selling to CBS had an inescapable logic in 1964, when Fender was incapable of satisfying demand for its guitars and needed a cash injection for new equipment.

'Leo and I had discussed the future of the company at the time,' says Don Randall. 'We'd grown to the point where we were going to have to put a lot more money into it, which neither of us at that time had, and feeling the way he did,

he felt he should extricate himself from it.'

By this time Leo, who it must be said was regarded by some of his colleagues as a hypochondriac, felt his health was suffering under the stress of running the company. Don remembers, 'Leo was a hypochondriac to begin with, he figured himself as being in poor health and was trying all kinds of phony medical things, going to chiropractors, drinking carrot juice . . . one time he drank so much carrot juice he turned orange.

'So I started looking at the options and after talking to our banker he suggested we talk to Merrill Lynch. Dean Woodman, who was head of the investment banking company at Merrill Lynch, thought we had a very saleable product and thought he could do a good job for us. In the meantime I had been contacted by the Baldwin Piano Company, and they wanted very badly to purchase the company, so I was dealing with two entities at the same time. And ultimately we sold to CBS because Baldwin wanted to buy us, but didn't want to pay for us!'

Don Randall conducted the negotiations with

CBS, which eventually agreed on a price of $13 million. CBS, which took over officially on January 1, 1965, was intent on maintaining standards at its new acquisition, and retained Leo Fender on a five-year consultancy contract, while Don Randall was also given a five-year contract as president of CBS Musical Instruments. Following the takeover, CBS invested in several new products: the Fender Electric XII, designed by Leo, came out in 1965 while the Fender line was expanded to include keyboards after Leo met Harold Rhodes, who had a design for a new electric piano. But although matters looked healthy at corporate level, the Fender staff who'd helped to establish the company felt alienated.

'The sale to CBS at first was kind of secretive, few of us knew much about it until it was almost finalized,' remembers George Fullerton. 'And I don't think it was accepted too well, a big company like CBS coming from New York to this area. Most people liked the way the company had been running, they were happy with the quality of the product – and most people don't like changes too much. And there certainly were a lot of changes after CBS came in. People left the company for various reasons, and, of course, CBS set up their own methods, brought in different people, new heads of departments, and that created controversy. I think at first the move was very good, they worked hard to maintain quality and did so for a long time, but eventually for more money and economy, pushed for more sales, and quality did drop.'

Some of the changes introduced in Fender guitars were intended to increase the quality of the product. A new form of truss rod, generally known as the 'bullet' truss rod, was introduced in 1971. This allowed the neck relief to be altered without removing the pickguard and was a real improvement. But later it was seen as the mark of a poor guitar because of the period with which it became associated. At the same time a new method of attaching the neck was introduced; now known as the 'three-bolt' method,

this allowed the angle of the neck to be altered relative to the body. According to George Fullerton, this neck joint was developed by Leo for the company's acoustic guitars and was applied to the electrics against his wishes. In any event, the neck joint was less rigid than the previous four-bolt method, and combined with the sloppy production standards that were starting to take hold, made the guitar less stable and affected the sound adversely. Although Leo Fender was still retained as a consultant by CBS, his involvement soon diminished, dealing a serious blow to the Fender brand, for Leo seemed to instinctively to grasp fundamentals of musical instrument design that eluded many of his rival designers. Leo's first guitar designs were workmanlike, reliable and solid, but as the CBS years rolled on the emphasis of the company's new products increasingly turned on gimmicks rather than genuine design features.

THE DEATH OF THE STRATOCASTER?

The British beat boom of the mid Sixties increased interest in guitar music generally. The most famous instruments of this era were the Gretsch guitars used by the Beatles and the Gibson Les Paul, which was adopted by a new breed of guitar hero, led by Eric Clapton, Jeff Beck, Peter Green and Paul Kossoff. So where did this leave the Strat? According to Bill Carson, destined for obsolescence: 'I was in marketing at the time. This was in '67, I think. I had started, along with some others, to pull raw materials and work in process down to a particular point. We had a target date, of October or whenever, for the last Stratocaster and the last Telecasters, because our Tele sales were way down, too.' Then the Hendrix album *Are You Experienced?* came out and sales went through the roof. But Forrest White, who was in charge of production at the time, describes this rumor as 'a bunch of crap', stating that Fender guitar sales were at a peak in the mid Sixties. Don Randall agrees: 'We never in the world considered dropping any of the guitars. We were selling too many of them, and we were continuing to expand the sales of the Telecaster and the Stratocaster.' In fact, although the Strat and the Tele were not the most high-profile guitars of the mid Sixties, they were probably the most sought-after electric guitars among professionals, and after the arrival of Jimi Hendrix they would remain unchallenged as two of the world's most popular guitars.

NEVER MIND THE QUALITY

Although any overnight differences between pre-CBS and CBS-era Fenders are largely the stuff of legend, by 1970 there were inescapable drops in the quality of the company's products. CBS ordered wood without specifying weight as a vital criterion – this resulted in guitars that were uncomfortably heavy. The importance of items such as the type of wire used for pickup coils was not fully understood, and the sound of the instruments changed as a result – to most observers, for the worse. Outside the guitar field, the situation was perhaps even more serious. Leo Fender's amplifiers, which were a vital and successful part of the product range, had up until now been exclusively tube-based designs. CBS pressed hard for a move to transistor-based circuitry, which was less labor-intensive to produce. Even at the time these early transistor amplifiers were recognized as dreadful, and among other consequences caused the loss of Forrest White, who'd overseen production at Fender for over a decade: 'I worked with CBS for over two years, but I refused to sign off some solid state amplifiers that were designed because I felt that they were not worthy of Leo Fender's name.' White quit in 1967. The deterioration in quality accelerated in 1969 when Randall resigned to form his own company. Leo Fender's original assistant, George Fullerton, departed in 1970. New machinery was brought in to increase guitar production in 1972. Sloppy programming resulted in a change of shape for both the Strat and Tele; the new body contours of the Strat gave the guitar a comparatively dumpy profile, while the actual outline shape of the Telecaster altered.

None of the production staff seemed either to notice or care about this obvious fault.

Undoubtedly the Seventies were Fender's worst years in terms of quality of output. The pressure caused by the bureaucracy of CBS was exacerbated by the increasing number of cheap guitars imported from Japan; Fender's student guitars were beginning to look overpriced, and the company went to some lengths to cut costs and introduce new, cheaper models such as the unsuccessful Bullet series. Even so, a policy of high margins helped Fender generate large profits for CBS, which reached $12.7 million by 1980. But from 1980 the sales started to dip, and a mythology was now established about earlier 'pre-CBS' instruments. Although attempts were made to return to basics by re-creating the old Strat shape with guitars such as 'The Strat', these failed to emulate the quality, or even the basic shape, of the company's earlier models. Eventually the CBS management recognized the extent to which Fender's reputation was suffering and, in 1981, head-hunted a new management team. Bill Schultz, who was hired as the Fender president, came from the Japanese Yamaha company:

'Fender was going through a bad time in the Eighties, after experiencing the success of the

Leo Fender receives an award from the Country Music Association in 1965, the year he officially sold the Fender company

music boom in the Seventies. At that time CBS
weren't putting money into R&D, into equipment,
or thinking about the future. The product began to
deteriorate, the quality was going down on all our
lines, and we were starting to feel it in the market-
place. I had no choice but to stop production completely, take everything out of our warehouses and
dealers' stores and run it back through our production line. It cost CBS a lot of money to do this,
but it put us in the right direction.'

Schultz recruited a new head of R&D, Dan
Smith, also from Yamaha, and started out on a
new model development program to bring the
range back to basics, returning to the old-fashioned four-bolt necks and small headstocks.
Schultz: 'I think it cost $1.3 million to stop pro-
duction, which, with due respect to CBS, they
allowed me to do. We improved the quality we
had, but the fit and the equipment and the finish
were just not what was expected out in the mar-
ketplace, especially since the Japanese had made an
entry to the market with a quality product. But we
struggled through and put a five-year program
together. I hired 30 to 35 R&D people, and we
developed a whole new catalogue of products.' At
the same time the company decided to fight fire
with fire, and to compete with foreign imports by
licensing Japanese Fenders. The Fender Japan
company was set up, owned jointly by Fender US
and two Japanese companies. This meant that
Fender could officially license copies and receive
income from copies which were sold in Japan;
shortly afterwards the company would also decide
to sell Japanese-made guitars in the US. Those
early Japanese guitars starkly pointed out the
problems facing Smith's team; the vintage reissues
produced by the Japanese seemed to be markedly
superior in quality to those on which the
American Fender staff was working: 'When we
saw them, we could have cried,' remembers Smith.

For the first time in a decade the quality of

*A sign of a return to the personal touch –
Fender president Bill Schultz in the Custom Shop*

Fender products started to noticeably improve; some designs, such as the Stratocaster Standard, signalled a return to the simplicity of the original concept, although other 'improvements', like the Elite which incorporated a new unwieldy vibrato system, were hardly welcomed.

By 1983 the increase in value of the American dollar created other problems, forcing the company to make cost-cutting changes such as dumping the Strat's distinctive dished jack plug socket. Despite the pressures, Schultz believed the company was on the verge of turning the corner. 'We were just starting to see the fruits of our labors when CBS decided to sell us. And at that time we just didn't know what to do; we had no money for advertising, we had no money for promotion, and our R&D program came to a halt. Eventually it was suggested by the treasurer of CBS that I put a group together and purchase Fender.'

For a time it looked as if the world's most influential guitar-maker was in real danger of going under. Although CBS discussed a straightforward sale of Fender to several other companies, most of the offers were comparatively derisory, while Bill Schultz himself experienced some considerable difficulty in attracting the necessary

The Esquier brand would later be adapted to Squier and applied to Japanese-made guitars instead of guitar strings

By 1979 Leo Fender spent much of his time yachting. (He would reportedly make several suggestions regarding yacht designs which would be incorporated by the manufacturers!)

investors: 'My chief financial officer put together a program, we took it out and pounded on the doors of all the banks, and believe me, no one was interested. The financial wizards wanted no part of us. However, as a last resort we found this little boutique investor in Chicago who believed in the people he met, believed in the name, and called a hundred dealers to see if they thought we could pull it off, and they said yes. He lent us the money we had to have, then we went to our major distributors and they invested in the company, then 13 people who worked for the company invested, and we finally put enough together to get started.' At the end of January 1985, just over two decades since the purchase of the company by CBS, a new era was about to start for Fender.

THE POST-CBS YEARS

Schultz's management team bought the Fender company for $12 million; considerably less in real terms than the $13 million paid for the operation in 1965. The deal did not include the existing Fender complex in Fullerton, which enjoyed a considerable real estate value, and for some time Schultz's team had no factory, few employees, a still-fluid product line and, according to Schultz, 'some of the assets we paid for were not good ones, let me tell you'. For much of 1985 Fender had to rely solely on Japanese-built guitars until a new factory in Corona, California, came on line.

Despite the dangers, it soon became obvious that the Fender name was enjoying a real rejuvenation, as announced by the American Standard Strat, launched in 1986. This was a subtle re-rendering of the initial concept, with a mildly improved tremolo that improved tuning stability while retaining the sound of the original. Still a mainstay of the American-made line, the American Standard is complemented by American-made vintage reissues, which seek to capture the flavor of '57- and '62-era instruments, and improved models such as the Strat Plus Deluxe which feature technical adjustments such as a tremolo system designed in conjunction with Floyd Rose – whose name is synonymous with modern trem systems – and Fender's Lace Sensor pickups. Perhaps more crucially, Fender is once again firmly committed to extensive collaborations with modern musicians, to produce guitars such as the Eric Clapton, Yngwie Malmsteen and Jeff Beck Signature Strats.

All of these player-developed instruments are the product of Fender's Custom Shop, which builds one-off models and short runs, as well as acting as an R&D center for the regular production line. Ironically, given the common misconception that pre-CBS Strats were made by hand, handmade Fender Strats are nowadays available at a price which, in real terms, is less than that of the factory originals in the Fifties. According to Schultz: 'Those guys in the Custom Shop can't wait to get into work in the morning – and that spirit makes its way through the whole company and the dealer network.

'In seven or eight years we have done a complete turnaround. The name Fender is one of the most esteemed brandnames in America, like Harley Davidson. And like Harley Davidson, we've been in trouble; we were both leverage buyouts, and we've both become very successful again.'

Measuring up to the past is never easy, and given that the original Strat of 1954 had such a dramatic effect on the course of music, it would be an incredible achievement to persuade players to value the modern guitars as highly as the vintage ones. Yet most of the Fender players who helped establish older instruments as the most collectible ones are now firm fans of the newer Custom Shop instruments. Magic is an elusive quality, and one that was sadly lacking in Fender guitars of the Seventies, but one that Fender now seem to have recaptured.

Almost uniquely, the Strat balances retro chic with absolute practicality, and as long as the electric guitar retains any importance in the music scene, there's no doubt that the model's future is assured. The icon is in safe hands.

THIS YEAR'S MODEL

Although recognizably the same guitar as when it was initially launched in 1954, the

Stratocaster has undergone many changes over the last 40 years which have affected its

playability and its collectibility.

The outline shape of the Stratocaster is as pleasing as it is familiar, but much of its appeal to guitarists lies in the details: hardtail or tremolo, rosewood or maple fingerboard, 'v' or 'u-shape' neck, two-tone sunburst or custom color. The Strat has continued to evolve since its launch in 1954 and has undergone many alterations in cosmetics or design, while still remaining demonstrably the

1956 Strat in the standard 'two-tone' sunburst finish

same guitar. All of these alterations have affected its value to guitarists and collectors.

The fact that the Strat's basic design has remained virtually unaltered since its inception is a good indication that Fender got it right the first time. Of the changes that have occurred over the past 40 years, some have proved beneficial, based on improved knowhow and associated production techniques, while others can be seen as detrimental, regrettably the result of financial dictates where quantity assumed priority over quality. Such good and bad aspects are not always specific to certain periods of manufacture, and individual merit often tends to be overlooked in the conveniently sweeping generalizations adopted within the vintage market, which means that instruments of different age attract widely varying levels of interest and associated values.

tion up to 1967, finds any obsession with serial numbers or exactly dating guitars laughable: 'When you read about how you can tell when a particular instrument was made by the dates and stuff, that's just not true. As an example, when we made out the nameplates we would just chuck them in a bin; and there'd be 5,000 of them. So you might have one guitar with one serial number, and another one with a serial number 400 or 500 higher – well, that guitar with the higher serial number could have been made four or five months before the other one.'

FENDER FICTION

As the Stratocaster has increased in popularity over the years, so has the folklore. In essence, the conception has arisen that old Strats are better than new ones. In his interview later in this book, Keith Richards makes a convincing argument for the magic of old guitars; but he also plays new ones, too. It's certainly true that the average late Fifties Strat is better made than the average late Seventies one, but individual guitars from a certain era can vary radically according to the pieces of wood used on that particular day, as well as the individual workmanship. Thus the following summary might indicate which models are most collectible – but it doesn't always follow that they're the best guitars. Fender was not making guitars for collectors, it was making them for musicians. Forrest White, who was head of Fender's produc-

THE COLLECTORS' MARKET

Over the past two decades the Stratocaster has become established as one of the world's most coveted electric guitars. Only the Les Paul is regarded as more collectible, partly because so few of the seminal late Fifties Standard models were made. But while at today's prices the very rarest Custom Color Fifties Strats are approaching the $50,000 mark, during the heyday of Jimi Hendrix the Strat had limited collectors' value – Eric Clapton and others have recounted that at the end of the Sixties early Strats could be had for a pittance. Norman Harris, of Norman's Rare Guitars in California, remembers that in the late Sixties: 'I was selling guitars, and at that time a pre-CBS rosewood neck Strat was fetching between $300 and $400. They're now fetching around $4000 for a guitar in original condition, and you can double that if it's exceptionally mint. There's an established market now, which is much like an art market – there are a lot of collectors who are very know-ledgeable and know exactly what they're

Vintage dealer Norm Harris and '62 Strat

looking for.'

As in any collectors' market, values have as much to do with rarity as inherent quality. Thus rare finishes attract premium prices, while originality is all-important. Working guitarists who have modified their instruments for practical purposes over the years will find that any alterations affect the guitar's value. Rick Nielsen of Cheap Trick remembers returning his '57 Strat to the Fender company in 1967 for repair: 'They did up the neck, changed the decal. No one ever thought in those days "Let's keep it like this." The mentality was, if it looks old let's make it look new.' By present-day standards the alterations to Rick's guitar were disastrous, but such is always the case with an artifact that changes from being a working tool to a work of art; meanwhile, the purchasers change, too. Norman Harris comments: 'I wouldn't say there's anyone collecting Stratocasters now who doesn't play the guitar. But whereas in the past the buyers might have been working musicians, now you also get guys who make a living as bankers or lawyers, who wanted a good guitar when they were kids, and now have the money to get one of the best.' Such is the downside of being an icon; like a pair of original Levi's that can't be worn, or a Harley that can't go out in the rain, objects that made their reputation as functional tools become commodities to be looked at, but not touched. Given the fact that a growing number of guitarists and collectors are chasing an ever-dwindling pool of instruments, it appears the escalation in prices of old Strats will continue until its 60th anniversary and later.

STRATOCASTERS THROUGH THE YEARS

Stratocaster production can be grouped into distinct periods, but it should be noted that the instruments in each group will inevitably vary. Unremitting consistency was, and still is, an impossible (and some would say unwelcome) ideal to achieve in guitar manufacture. Instruments that have become more valuable than others aren't necessarily intrinsically superior; indeed, a well-worked guitar which has lost its original finish, while possessing a tiny price tag compared with its unplayed contemporary, will in all likelihood be a better guitar.

The following listing records the 40-year evolution of the Stratocaster. For ease of reference the 'standard' version has been assigned to six production eras. All dates shown are approximate

and are offered for guidance only, as there were no definite simultaneous cut-off or start-up points for the changes noted. As Forrest White observed, changes were not made wholesale and in one sweep but invariably were introduced over a period, often overlapped and resulted in instruments in which various combinations of old and new features could be found.

1. 1954–59 'PRE-CBS'

DESCRIPTION: One-piece maple neck with 'integral' fingerboard (21 frets inserted directly into the radiused top surface). Small headstock carrying a thin-script (nicknamed 'spaghetti') gold Fender logo, in addition to a small guide for the top E and B strings to provide adequate

1955 'two-tone' Strat

downward tension at the nut.

Six metal button Kluson machine heads located along the left side of the headstock, with base-plates cut down to fit.

Contrasting black dot markers on front and side of neck.

Blonde '73 Strat, as owned by Yngwie Malmsteen

Adjustable truss rod fitted in neck, with a recessed adjuster located at the body end.

A contrasting strip of wood (or 'skunk stripe') fills the channel cut in the back of the neck to accommodate the truss-rod.

Neck secured to the body with four screws mounted through a metal plate ('four-bolt' neck).

Ash or alder wood body, with two offset cutaways and horns. Heavily beveled away on the front under the guitarist's forearm, with similar beveling in the waist area on the back.

Single-layer white plastic pickguard secured to the body with eight screws. Some were made of anodized aluminium instead.

Three pickguard-mounted single-coil pickups, each with six staggered-height magnet polepieces visible through a white plastic cover. One situated near the end of the neck; one near the bridge, angled for bass/treble emphasis; the third located centrally.

Controls are also mounted on the pickguard, comprising one volume and two tone, with white plastic knobs carrying the appropriate legends. The volume control acts over all pickups, while the first tone relates to the neck pickup, the second to the middle unit. A three-position lever switch (of a type used in juke boxes) selects either neck, middle or bridge pickups.

The bridge provides height and intonation adjustment for each string, with six pressed steel saddles mounted on a metal base plate fixed to a steel inertia block as part of the built-in vibrato tailpiece. The latter uses a maximum of five tension-adjustable springs, located in a cavity on the back of the body under a white plastic cover plate. A screw-in bent metal arm provides the vertical leverage necessary to operate the vibrato unit.

The non-vibrato equipped version (nicknamed 'hardtail') uses the same six saddles but on a metal base plate secured to the body front.

Strings are rear-loaded on both versions, either anchored in the inertia block of the vibrato unit, or in ferrules located in the body back of the non-vibrato model.

Output jack socket located in a recessed plate mounted on the front of the body.

Two strap buttons, both mounted on the side of the body, one on the top of the left horn, the other in the center of the body base.

Body finished in two-tone sunburst as standard.

There was no tone control for the bridge pick-up, the intention being the ability to provide maximum variation between the three units with speedy changeover from rhythm to solo settings.

No combined settings were 'officially' obtainable on the three-way selector switch. Fender considered that the three choices provided offered enough tonal variety, thanks to the well-considered locations of the pickups. However, players soon found that the lever could be lodged between the 'official' positions.

VARIANTS

Strats of this period were reasonably standardized, although the company experimented with different forms of plastics for early control knobs and pickup covers. The earliest guitars used a brittle and more damage-prone white phrenolic plastic, similar to Bakelite, for early pickup covers, around 1954–5. Early Strats feature round string retainers, which in 1956 changed to the 'butterfly' type.

Custom Color Strats, some with gold fittings, were made from the instrument's very early days, and, in the beginning, only for those guitarists known to the Fender factory, such as Eldon Shamblin and Alvino Rey; not surprisingly, they are particularly rare. The standard finish changed to a three-tone sunburst

around 1958, although the red has faded away on some early examples.

SOUND & COLLECTIBILITY

The sound of the Strats of this period are considered by many to differ from year to year. Some guitarists reckon, for example, that the '56 has a drier tone than the sweeter-sounding '58. However, it should be remembered that the pickups used on all these oldies were hand-wound on primitive equipment, resulting in significant differences in tone and output. This factor alone is probably

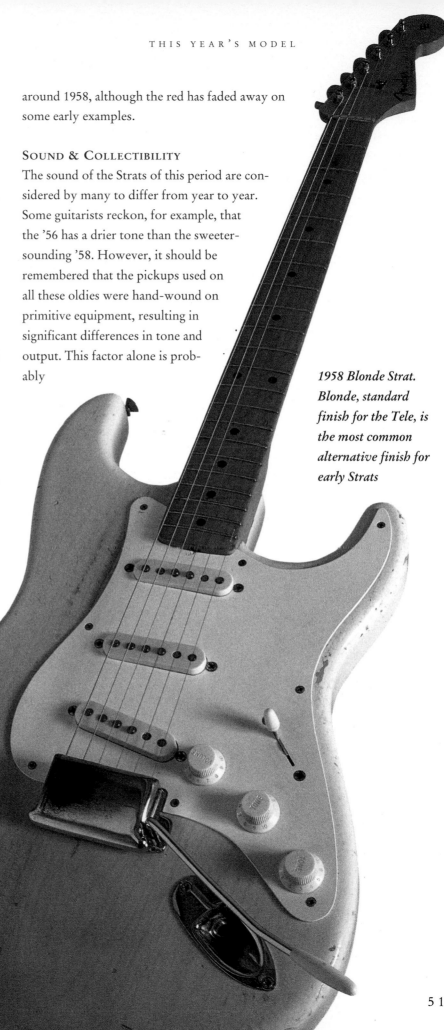

1958 Blonde Strat. Blonde, standard finish for the Tele, is the most common alternative finish for early Strats

*The front and back
shot of this 1958 Strat
clearly shows the
severe contouring of
the early models*

responsible for the fact that no two Strats of this period sound the same. Choice of woods also affects tone, as does the lengthy aging process (over at least three decades). Just about the only consistent tonal aspect is the small degree of treble emphasis provided by the lacquered maple 'fingerboard'. Neck 'feels' certainly vary throughout this period; most early guitars feature a fairly bulky round neck, while '56 or '57 necks have a distinctive 'V' profile, which is often referred to as a 'boat' neck. These early guitars tend to be far more comfortable in weight terms than Seventies Fenders, coming in at around 7.5 lb (3.4 kg) for a typical example.

Early Fifties Strats are the most collectible Fenders. Prices are volatile, and for many instruments of this period demand has exceeded supply, doubling prices between '91 and '94. At the beginning of the decade $8000 would have been a respectable price for a two-tone sunburst example in good condition; in 1995 the same guitar might fetch from $12,000 to $25,000. As for Custom Color guitars of this era, according to Norman Harris: 'They're so rare that they might fetch from $15,000 up to $30,000 or even $40,000 for a good example with gold-plated parts.' If the market continues its current trend, the $50,000 Strat will soon be with us.

2. 1959–65 'PRE-CBS SIXTIES'

DESCRIPTION: Similar to the 1954–59 'Pre-CBS Fifties', except:

Maple neck with separate glued-on rosewood fingerboard. Until mid 1963 the latter was a thick type with a flat base (nicknamed 'slab board') mated to a similarly shaped surface on the neck. This can be discerned when the latter is viewed from the body end, the join between fingerboard and neck being a straight line. From mid 1962 the rosewood fingerboard was thinner with the base radiused to match the top (nicknamed 'veneer board') and the surface of the maple neck shaped accordingly. George Fullerton maintains this change was intended to increase stability in the varying climates to which the guitar would be subjected, as well as improving the tone by effectively coupling the frets directly to the maple of the neck.

White 'clay' dot markers on front and side of fingerboard.

No contrasting wood strip on the back of the neck; the separate fingerboard construction enables the truss-rod to be front-mounted.

Triple-layer white/black/white laminated plastic pickguard secured to the body with 11 screws.

Finished in three-tone sunburst as standard.

1956 Blonde Strats with gold fittings. (These Strats are often termed 'Mary Kaye' models, as the celebrated guitarist was pictured with a blonde guitar in Fifties catalogues)

VARIANTS

Custom Color Strats are more common in this era, although still far outnumbered by the standard finish. A few guitars have celluloid pickguards with a tortoiseshell pattern.

SOUND & COLLECTIBILITY

The unlacquered rosewood fingerboard imparts a warmer overall tonality; more apparent on examples up to mid 1963 which have the thicker type. This is probably the only meaningful generalization that can be made about Strats of this era; as before, each guitar should be judged on its merits. One noted difference in this series of guitar is the

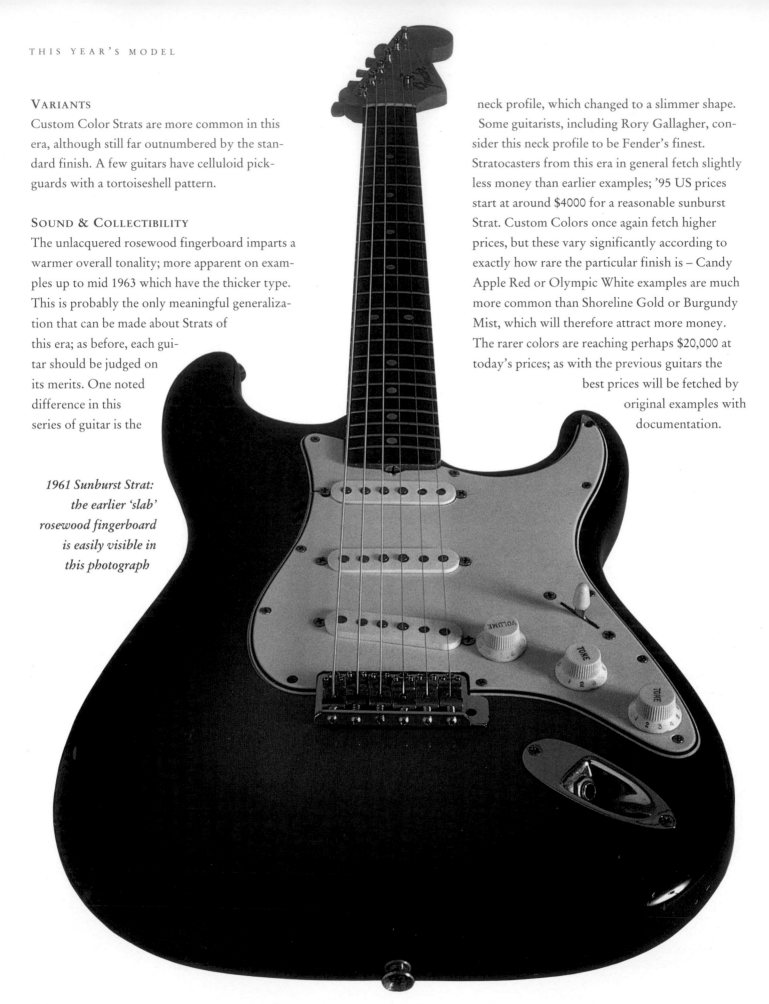

1961 Sunburst Strat: the earlier 'slab' rosewood fingerboard is easily visible in this photograph

neck profile, which changed to a slimmer shape. Some guitarists, including Rory Gallagher, consider this neck profile to be Fender's finest. Stratocasters from this era in general fetch slightly less money than earlier examples; '95 US prices start at around $4000 for a reasonable sunburst Strat. Custom Colors once again fetch higher prices, but these vary significantly according to exactly how rare the particular finish is – Candy Apple Red or Olympic White examples are much more common than Shoreline Gold or Burgundy Mist, which will therefore attract more money. The rarer colors are reaching perhaps $20,000 at today's prices; as with the previous guitars the best prices will be fetched by original examples with documentation.

1962 Sonic Blue guitar: although not the rarest Custom Color, Sonic Blue is a fashionable shade which now commands a hefty price premium over its sunburst counterparts

1962 Olympic White Strat: this finish ages in many different ways depending on how well the original paint was sealed, and can vary from brilliant white to an almost yellow color

1964 Candy Apple Red Stratocaster: This finish appeared the previous year. Some rare guitars feature matching painted headstocks, which increase their value

The wear on this 1971 Candy Apple Red clearly shows the separate filler and metallic undercoat used to produce the metallic finish

This blonde 1967 Strat is one of Yngwie Malmsteen's stage instruments

3. 1965–71 'CBS Sixties'

DESCRIPTION: Similar to the 1959–65 'Pre-CBS Sixties', except:

Headstock with a similar outline but enlarged on the right-hand side, helping to counteract the warping problems which could occur on the earlier small type. By this time the Fender logo is in a thicker script, changing from gold to black in 1968.

Pearloid dot markers.

Maple fingerboard option offered from 1967, again with no contrasting wood strip on the back of the neck. Replaced in 1970 by the reintroduction of the one-piece maple neck with 'integral' fingerboard.

Metal button machine heads with angled baseplates and the Fender 'F' stamped on each cover from 1967.

Body contouring reduced.

SOUND & COLLECTIBILITY

These early CBS instruments featured only minor changes compared to their more esteemed pre-CBS counterparts, yet both players and collectors have tended to overlook them. Models tended to feature bulkier 'U' shaped necks, which some players dislike. The guitar itself was becoming heavier, and the lack of body contouring and larger headstock were tending to detract from the Strat's cosmetics. A change from the original nitro-cellulose finishes, around 1967, prevented the guitars from eventually gaining the finely crazed patina loved by many fans. Even so, many of the Stratocasters produced in this period are fine instruments. They were also the type preferred by Jimi Hendrix, who played the glued-on maple fingerboard version almost exclusively.

As the supply of pre-CBS instruments has dwindled, these Strats have begun to gain more respect. Even so, there is a distinct divide in values between, say, a '64 Strat and a '66; the latter would be worth 40 percent less than its pre-CBS cousin.

Jimi Hendrix's Woodstock guitar fetched $297,000

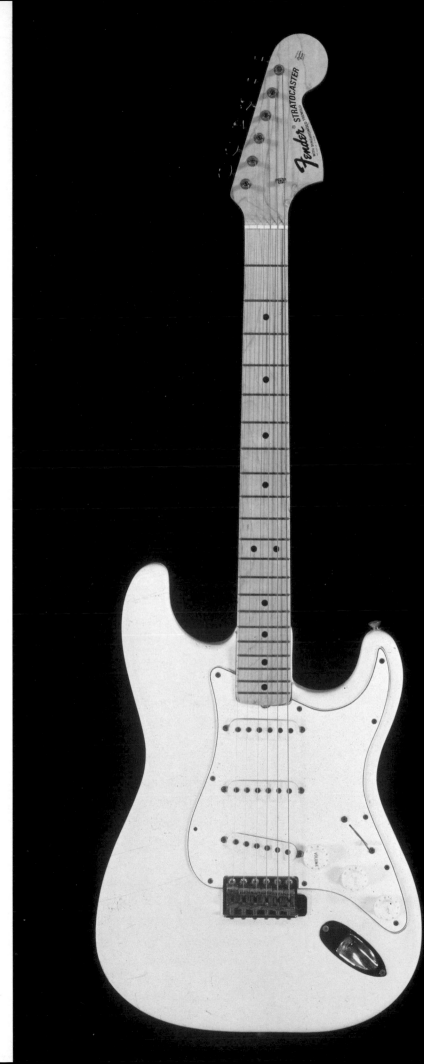

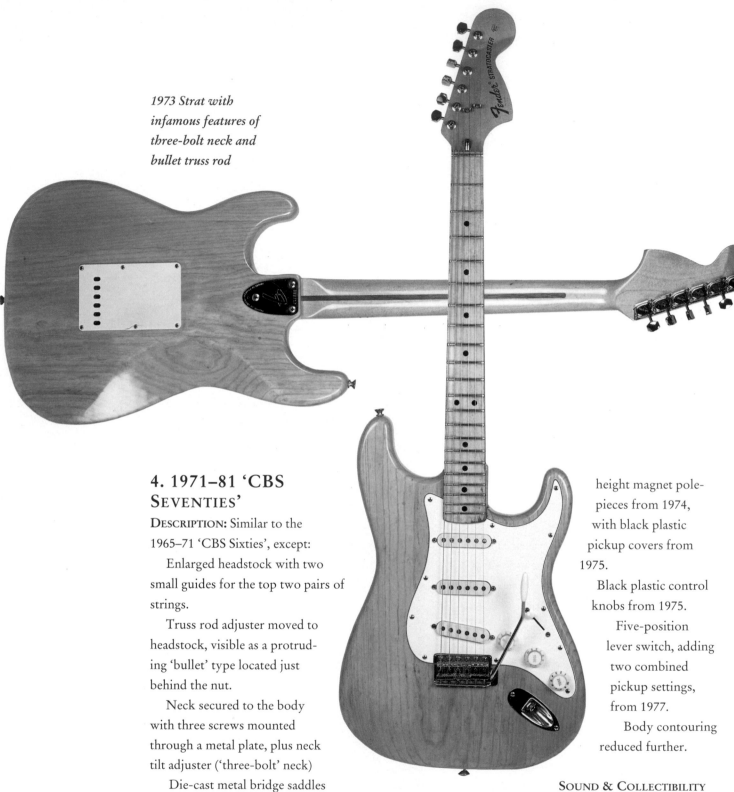

1973 Strat with infamous features of three-bolt neck and bullet truss rod

4. 1971–81 'CBS SEVENTIES'

DESCRIPTION: Similar to the 1965–71 'CBS Sixties', except:

Enlarged headstock with two small guides for the top two pairs of strings.

Truss rod adjuster moved to headstock, visible as a protruding 'bullet' type located just behind the nut.

Neck secured to the body with three screws mounted through a metal plate, plus neck tilt adjuster ('three-bolt' neck)

Die-cast metal bridge saddles mounted on a die-cast metal base plate with integral inertia block for the vibrato unit.

Triple-layer black/white/black laminated plastic pickguard from 1975.

Three single coil pickups each with six equal-height magnet pole-pieces from 1974, with black plastic pickup covers from 1975.

Black plastic control knobs from 1975.

Five-position lever switch, adding two combined pickup settings, from 1977.

Body contouring reduced further.

SOUND & COLLECTIBILITY

It is this period of Stratocaster which attracts most denigration; although some of the guitar's new features had practical value, this was often offset by indifferent manufacturing quality.

The necessity for the string guide on the third

This Seventies Strat has had a left-handed neck fitted by owner Yngwie Malmsteen

and fourth strings is questionable, as it increases tension and friction in the critical headstock area, leading to tuning problems. The relocated truss rod adjuster certainly made life easier, as the neck no longer had to be removed to execute appropriate adjustments.

The three-bolt neck could certainly work if applied correctly, as demonstrated on Music Man and G&L instruments. But Fender drilled over-large holes through the body, allowing undue movement of the neck-fixing screws, regardless of whether three or four were employed. The new neck tilt adjuster was also included to make setting-up faster and easier. Unfortunately, thanks to the production problems inherent in the three-bolt neck fixing system, it tended to make matters worse.

The change from steel to die-cast metal for the bridge/vibrato unit was certainly for the worse, in terms of tone, sustain and longevity – a classic

instance of financial considerations taking precedence over product quality. The pickups with equal height magnet polepieces generally sound inferior to previous types, lacking in volume and tonal range. The reduction in body contouring was another cost-cutting measure, reducing work on the production line. These guitars are also among the heaviest Strats; some designers at the time thought, incorrectly, that heavier wood gave improved sustain, but this change probably arose because tighter selection of woods would increase costs.

Despite all the drawbacks of these much maligned guitars, it's still quite possible to find a good example. Bluesman Walter Trout describes his '73 non-trem as 'a gem – I wouldn't sell it for a million dollars', while Rory Gallagher was surprised to find that another '73 guitar held its own against vintage examples in side-by-side tests. While Fender definitely produced some of its worst-ever guitars during this period, these Seventies models can often surpass their reputation. Perhaps the tacky shiny natural finishes will one day again become regarded, like tie-dyes or patchouli oil, as the height of fashion. In the meantime, current values for this period of Stratocaster are languishing below the $1000 mark.

5. 1981–84 'CBS EIGHTIES'
STANDARD (1ST VERSION) 1981–83
DESCRIPTION: Although succeeding the 'CBS Seventies' version, some aspects of styling and features have more in common with earlier predecessors:

The headstock reverts to a small size, but still with black Fender logo and two string guides.

Recessed truss-rod adjuster located at body end of neck.

Neck secured to the body with four screws mounted through a metal plate, no neck tilt adjuster.

21 frets.

Triple-layer white/black/white laminated plastic pickguard.

1981 'Gold-on-Gold' Strat

White plastic pick-up covers.

White control knobs.

Significantly increased contouring on front and back of body.

This model marked a conscious effort by Fender to return the Stratocaster to earlier standards of design and production. To an extent this succeeded, and examples do offer improvements in appearance and performance. So far they've not attracted the interest of collectors.

STANDARD (2ND VERSION) 1983–84

DESCRIPTION: Similar to the 1981–83 Standard, except:

Silver Fender logo.

Metal button machine heads with Fender stamped on each die-cast metal casing.

Truss rod adjuster on headstock, located in a recess just behind the nut.

Single-layer white plastic pickguard secured to the body with 12 screws.

Controls also mounted on the pickguard, comprising volume and tone, with white plastic knobs carrying the appropriate legends.

Revised-design six-saddle bridge/vibrato unit using tension-adjustable springs located under the pickguard. A push-in bent metal arm provides the vertical leverage necessary to operate the vibrato unit.

Strings are top-loaded, anchored in the bridge plate of the vibrato unit.

Output jack socket located on pickguard.

The cost-cutting features displayed on this version departed from the traditional design and detracted from its appeal. Examples play well and sound fine, but the vibrato unit has inherent design problems and can prove very temperamental.

VINTAGE REISSUES 1982–84

Reissues of the 1957-period and 1962-period originals (although not authentic re-creations) originating from a time when Fender at last became aware of the demand for vintage-style instruments, and the competition from overseas. These models offer some of the character aspects of the oldies combined with good quality and performance, in a much more affordable package than the 'real thing'.

6. 1986–CURRENT 'FMI'

AMERICAN STANDARD 1986–PRESENT DAY

DESCRIPTION: similar to Standard (1st version), except:

Silver Fender logo.

Metal button machine heads with Fender stamped on each die-cast metal casing.

Twenty-two frets.

Truss rod adjuster on headstock, located in a recess just behind the nut.

Neck secured to the body with four screws mounted through a metal plate, plus neck tilt adjuster.

Revised-design bridge/vibrato unit is similar to original design, but with subtle improvements, including powder-coated cast stainless steel saddles and two fulcrum points.

This model of the American Standard was a successful update of the Stratocaster theme; although eminently affordable for an American-built instrument it has gained many fans among professionals, including Johnny Marr.

VINTAGE 1985–CURRENT

The '57 and '62 re-issues continued under the auspices of the new company, providing the 'vintage alternative' (with attendant pros and cons) to the

The current American Standard is a subtle – and successful – update of the Strat theme

American Standard model.

RECENT VARIANTS

In addition to the 'standard' incarnations of the Stratocaster, there have been numerous production variants. These roughly fall into four categories:

'*Special*' models: Upmarket versions of the Strat theme.

1980–83 The Strat
1981–83 Gold-on-Gold
1983–84 Elite
1987–current Strat Plus
1990–current US Strat Ultra
1992-current Set-neck

Improvements to the Plus Deluxe include locking machine heads, Lace Sensor pickups, TBX tone control and a Fender/Floyd Rose vibrato system

'*Anniversary*' models: Official commemoration of various birthdays during the Strat's long-running existence.

1979–80 25th Anniversary
1990–91 35th Anniversary
1994 40th Anniversary/40th Anniversary Concert Edition

'*Artist Signature*' models: Most of these guitars originated as Custom Shop models. Although most of them differ in flavor, featuring perhaps active midboosts (Clapton Strat), scalloped frets (Malmsteen) or bridge humbucker (Beck), all remain reasonably faithful to the original Strat

concept and will probably have future appeal to collectors.

1988–current Eric Clapton
1988–current Yngwie Malmsteen
1991–current Jeff Beck
1992–current Robert Cray
1992–current Stevie Ray Vaughan
1992–current Hank Marvin
1993–current Richie Sambora

Fender's Signature model Strats incorporate improvements suggested by their endorsees. From top, the Clapton Strat is a Fifties-style guitar based on 'Blackie' but with Lace Sensor pickups and a hefty gain boost. The Stevie Ray Vaughan model is more conventional with vintage-sounding 'Texas overwound' pickups. The Hank Marvin model is based on Hank's original red guitar with subtle improvements such as a graphite nut. Jeff Beck's signature guitar features a twin Gold Lace Sensor combination in bridge position, and a roller nut. Richie Sambora's guitar has the Floyd Rose vibrato unit while Yngwie Malmsteen's Signature guitar is traditional except for its 'scalloped' fingerboard

'Hot Rod' models: Contemporary versions aimed at the metal market, sporting requisite features such as humbucker pickups and locking vibratos.

1989–90 HM Strat
1989–91 US Contemporary
1990–92 HM Strat Ultra
1992–current Floyd Rose Classic
1992–current Set-neck Floyd Rose

OVERSEAS STRATOCASTERS

Fender Japan was set up in 1982 to combat increasing competition from abroad, and it has proved to be a great success. The guitars made there offer quality and value for money, deservedly becoming the brand leaders in their field. Many Fender Japan instruments are intended for the domestic market only, but some do reach a wider audience.

In 1982 Fender decided to revive the Squier brand name. This was initially allotted to export lines of instruments made by Fender Japan, prior to being joined by the Fender-branded versions. The Squier Stratocasters of 1982–84 were very good reproductions of the '57 and '62 period American originals, and provided both inspiration and benchmark for the US-made reissues. Many famous players preferred to play Squier Stratocasters, leaving their high-value American oldies safe and secure at home.

Korean Squiers appeared in 1985, joining the on-going Japanese selection, and Mexican versions followed six years later. Such a range of production sources guarantees blanket coverage of most markets, and indeed the Stratocaster, in its many guises, has become the dominant model around the world.

THE CUSTOM SHOP

Fender's Custom Shop provides perhaps the most exciting products for future collectors. Set up in 1987, it produces small production runs and one-off custom models, which tend to be either extra-fastidious vintage re-creations, or hybridized modernized guitars. Without a doubt these guitars

have gained Fender new kudos; their credibility is perhaps indicated by the fact that vintage dealer Norman Harris sells Custom Shop models alongside his highly-priced vintage guitars: 'We've commissioned a range in unusual colors, with the matching headstocks, and they go very well with the original Fifties and Sixties guitars. They're bound to become collectors' items in the future.'

Fender has produced two sets of limited edition models commemorating the Stratocaster's 40th Anniversary. The 1954 Strat features the authentic two-tone finish and construction, and comes complete with a reproduction of the rare original-shaped case as well as a repro of the original guarantee and handbook. The production run is 1954 examples. Even rarer is the 40th Anniversary run of just 40 Ruby Custom Color guitars with gold fittings, made by the Custom Shop's Jay Black. Number One of this edition was recently sold at auction in London for $48,000.

The Custom Shop's John Page with the Phoenix Strat

The Limited Edition chrome Harley Davidson
Strat is intended to emphasize the two
companies' similar status as American icons

This flame maple Strat
is typical of the
Custom Shop's
handcrafted output

This white Strat with
tortoiseshell
pickguard and
matching headstock
evokes a vintage feel,
while the gold 'Dick
Dale' model
incorporates a
left-hand neck

*40th Anniversary
Concert Edition*

*Only 1954 examples of
the '1954' anniversary
guitar will be made.
All come with a
vintage-style case and
handbook*

*Serial numbers 2
and 3 of the 40th
Anniversary Concert
Edition*

*Opposite: No 1 40th Anniversary Concert Edition,
which made £32,000 ($ 52,800) when it was sold at
auction in London in 1994*

THE FENDER INFLUENCE

The influence of the Fender Stratocaster is under-
lined by the number of manufacturers who have
chosen to copy it. From guitars which have been
influenced by the Strat to models which set out to
be exact replicas, Fender has spawned a whole
industry. Rather than diminishing in significance
over the years, the Strat's influence has actually
increased to the point where practically every one
of Fender's rivals produces an obvious derivative.

Leo Fender's early guitar designs were so
groundbreaking that it's not really surprising that
rival manufacturers chose to launch their own
version: thus Gibson, Gretsch and others launched

*George Harrison's
Futurama was one of
the first guitars
aimed to evoke a
'Fender' feel*

solid body electrics in the wake of the Telecaster,
while Fender's Precision Bass also inspired countless interpretations. But the Stratocaster was
arguably the first Fender to have its cosmetics, as
well as its basic concept, copied. By the end of the
Fifties several European makers were offering
streamlined guitars obviously inspired by the
Strat, and as interest in the electric guitar grew so
more makers moved in. By 1963 guitars such as
the Selmer Futurama were being bought by
George Harrison and others as a substitute for the
real thing. Major manufacturers, including Hofner
from Germany and Italy's Eko, produced obvious
derivatives, while other makers such as Vox and
Burns in England and Mosrite in the US were
producing instruments which, while boasting
original touches, set out to replicate the functions
of the Strat with generally similar cosmetics and a
tremolo system.

Yet while the Strat's influence was already significant in these early days, as time passed its
effect on other manufacturers would become even
more profound, and their imitations more and
more slavish. By the early Seventies Japanese companies were producing cosmetically identical
copies of the Strat, under brandnames such as
Antoria and Ibanez; eventually, as the copy craze
continued, practically every important American
guitar design would be replicated, but the Strat
was by far the most popular recipient of this
dubious accolade. Ironically, Strat copies were
optimized for mass production, and they tended
to be better instruments than Gibson Les Paul or
ES-335 copies. By 1980 Japanese companies such as
Tokai and Fernandes were producing painstakingly
accurate replicas of vintage Fenders that were
closer in feel and sound to the original than the
contemporary Fender product. This was a major
factor in the company's decision to set up Fender
Japan.

Copy guitars have become so commonplace that
the practice is now seen as completely respectable.
Fender is unfortunate, compared with other international companies, in that the copying of older

guitar designs is now difficult to prevent. Under most laws in Europe, for example, the fact that copies have been in existence for around 20 years precludes legal measures against them. In America Fender has forced copyists to depart from the classic Strat headstock shape, which is now regarded as a visual trademark. This has not, however, deterred rivals from producing otherwise identical copies, while even comparatively innovative manufacturers, for instance the American Peavey company, are now producing copies of the Stratocaster and Telecaster.

There is, of course, a supreme irony in the fact that the Strat's superlative design has forced manufacturers to abandon originality and opt for imitation; both Fender, and perhaps the guitar market in general, have suffered as a consequence. Yet there are companies that, while retaining the Strat sound as a benchmark, have assimilated the Strat's design principles into their own instruments; even makers such as Ibanez, which started out making barefaced copies, have lately turned to more distinctive designs. But there are very few guitar companies that do not include a Strat lookalike, or soundalike, in their line: both the sound and look of the Strat have now become standard. Even the company's long-standing rival, Gibson, has turned to Strat-copies in its Korean-made Epiphone line. While these derivatives have doubtless cost Fender sales, they have also helped ensure the continuance of the Strat's dominance, for any budding guitarist knows that a cheap copy can only be a temporary stop on the way to the real thing. For the guitar they dream about will have 'Fender' on the headstock.

This 1970 'Top Twenty' budget guitar was one of countless instruments which imitated Fender cosmetics – but any sonic resemblance to the real thing was extremely remote

CHAPTER SIX

STRAT APPEAL

Although the Stratocaster was a technical tour de force, it would never have reached its present

popularity without its use by countless high-profile players. Some guitarists, such as Jimi

Hendrix or Eric Clapton, extracted sounds from it Leo Fender surely could not have imagined.

In 1954 the Stratocaster looked like a guitar from another planet. The Telecaster, made out of a slab of wood, was one thing, but the Strat, with its horns, body contours, glossy finish and flash gadgetry looked like something out of Buck Rogers. The first time they saw it, most musicians shied away from the new instrument – it was so new-fangled that few could see themselves playing it. For the guitar to succeed it needed some high-profile players who would help it reach aspirational status. That would come with a new form of music: rock 'n' roll.

Buddy Holly and the Crickets

Fender executives had never heard of a young kid called Buddy Holly when he first arrived on the scene in 1957, but Holly's first album, *The "Chirping" Crickets*, was a huge milestone for the new guitar. The album cover, which showed Holly holding his early sunburst Strat, was the best piece of publicity the company could have asked for, and for a huge number of players, including Hank Marvin, Eric Clapton and Jeff Beck, this was the first time they had seen the new instrument. But the excitement wasn't only visual, for Holly popularized the sound of a small rock 'n' roll combo – guitar, vocals, bass and drums – which would become the standard for rock music.

Although Leo Fender and his associates had no idea that the Stratocaster would be used for new musical forms such as rock 'n' roll, it would turn out to be perfectly suited to it. The same thing would happen nearly a decade later, when a young guitarist called James Marshall Hendrix burst onto the British music scene. His use of the Stratocaster would prove even more influential than Buddy Holly's.

Hendrix's guitar playing and his onstage antics might have horrified some of the Fender staff, but his music provided the perfect demonstration of the ultimate capabilities of the Strat, which at the time was being overshadowed by the Gibson

Jimi Hendrix (opposite) – single-handedly responsible for the late Sixties' resurgence of the Strat

guitars used by the likes of Eric Clapton and Peter Green. Firstly, by pairing the Strat with a British-made Marshall amplifier, Hendrix created a whole new palette of tones. Hendrix's playing incorporated tricks learned from blues, rock, soul and country and western, and the Stratocaster was capable of letting him express all of these shadings. The Stratocaster could be used for brutal power chords and lead riffs, as well as for subtle melodic lines – hearing Hendrix, guitarists realized that the Stratocaster could accommodate a lifetime's worth of guitar tricks.

From Buddy Holly to Jimi Hendrix, Dick Dale to Stevie Ray Vaughan, it was musicians who made the Strat's reputation. However good the guitar design, if the right guitar players hadn't latched onto it, the Strat wouldn't have been successful. But by a gradual process, as one musician alerted another to the guitar's possibilities, the world's electric guitarists took to Fender's most popular instrument.

Sonny Curtis

THE MODERN STRATPACK

The Stratocaster would have been stillborn without players who could unleash its potential. In many ways the story of the Strat has been the story of the uses to which it has been put, and from the time guitarists first discovered that they could lodge its pickup switch at positions between those designed for it, the guitar has been used in ways which Leo Fender could not have envisioned.

The Stratocaster is more than a musical instrument – it's a soulmate, an obsession, a comforter, an inspiration. Every Stratpacker has a story to tell about his guitar, and for almost every one of the guitarists interviewed for this book, the moment they first cast eyes on the Strat has lodged in their memory. Here are some of the countless musicians for whom the Strat is irreplaceable, describing in their own words what makes it special.

SONNY CURTIS played with Buddy Holly in the Crickets, and would later play with Bobby Vee and the Everly Brothers.
'I first met Buddy Holly back in Lubbock, Texas, when he and I were both in high school. This friend of mine took me over to his house, and we didn't get into small talk or anything – we just went straight into playing music. We were mainly into bluegrass and country music. Then we fell into listening to Elvis Presley, then along came Little Richard, Fats Domino, Ray Charles – he was a little more sophisticated, we couldn't figure out some of his chords – and, of course, Chuck Berry. At the outset, we couldn't listen to that music 'cause it was considered race music. We'd have to go out in the car late at night and listen to this show out of Shreveport, Louisiana, which played the greatest music in the world. I used to spend the night with Holly, we'd go out at midnight and sit in his car, and fall asleep listening to the music.

'Buddy bought a Stratocaster way before the Crickets. I don't know why he bought one, and don't know if it was just a vision or what. I had a D–28 Martin, and I had seen a Stratocaster or two in music stores, but I wouldn't have bought one myself because it was a sort of futuristic-looking thing and I would have been scared of it. Matter of fact, a little later on I bought a Byrdland, which was produced by Gibson, a kind of a jazz guitar, and the problem with it was that you couldn't play loud enough with it to suit me, because it would feed back. Now that was the beauty of the Stratocaster – you could turn that thing up where you could blow the back end out of a building and it wouldn't feed back on you, and of course we liked that because we loved to play loud.

'I only met Leo Fender one time, when we were fixing to do a Bobby Vee meets the Crickets tour in England in 1962. Our manager thought this was a big enough deal that we might be able to get some free instruments if we went out to Fender Instruments in Fullerton. So we're going through the factory, we'd picked out some guitars

that we'd liked, and these guys are saying to our manager, "No, we don't do that sort of thing. It doesn't matter who you are, we do not give instruments away. We may give you a discount, but there's no way we'll give you any free instruments." And all of a sudden this guy walked up,

---

'**THE BEAUTY OF THE STRATOCASTER WAS THAT YOU COULD TURN THAT THING UP WHERE YOU COULD BLOW THE BACK END OUT OF A BUILDING AND IT WOULDN'T FEED BACK ON YOU. AND OF COURSE WE LIKED THAT, BECAUSE WE LOVED TO PLAY LOUD.'**

---

and I was sitting there picking something on the guitar, and this guy says, "Why don't you give these boys what they need for the trip." Well these guys didn't know what to think, they said, "You know it's not our policy to give guitars away." And he said, "I'll tell you what, just let them borrow them – and they won't ever have to give 'em back!" And that was Leo Fender. He actually gave me that guitar, it's a great old guitar, and I'm really proud of it.'

DICK DALE was a pioneer of surf music and along with Buddy Holly was one of the first prominent users of the Strat in the pop world.
'I met Leo in 1955. I was playing some old handmade guitar that I'd bought from a pawnshop in Los Angeles, and my father and I went straight up to Leo, and I told him, "My name's Dick Dale. I don't really have a guitar, and I'm going to start playing in this place called the Rendezvous in Balboa." And he took a liking to me, gave me a Stratocaster and said, "Take this and fool around with it, and take this amplifier. Keep beating on

Dick Dale

'Leo used to say, "When it's fit for Dick Dale's barrages and punishments, it is then fit for human consumption".'

them and tell me what you think of both of them."

'Now when I met Leo in the mid Fifties I didn't know of any groups except the country players – all the different cities weren't even issuing licences to have teenage dancing. So my dad and I, we were the first, we'd go and meet the teachers, the police and the fire department to organize these shows. And these people told us, "They gotta wear ties!" So we had to get boxes of ties and hand them out to the kids at the door. At the Rendezvous we started off with 17 surfers and ended up with 4,000 people a night. All these kids like the Beach Boys, Jan and Dean and the Righteous Brothers would come and check us out.

'Now when we were playing these places all those people in there would just suck up the

sound. At the time Leo was just making amplifiers for country players with 10-inch speakers and I kept blowing them up; they'd catch on fire and I must have blown up about 48 of them. So I got Leo down to the hall, him and Freddie Tavares, and they stood in this audience of 4,000 people and Leo said to Freddie, "Now I know what Dick Dale's trying to tell me." So he went back to the drawing board, and the final result was the Showman amplifier, with a big 15-inch Lansing speaker, and then we ended up with the Dual Showman, with twin 15-inch speakers. Leo used to say, "When it's fit for Dick Dale's barrages and punishments, it is then fit for human consumption." I used to get a kick out of hearing that.

'When Leo gave me my guitar, it was a right-handed guitar, and I'm left-handed. I played it upside down, backwards. Then I asked Leo if he could put the controls down here, 'cause I'm always shutting them off and I'd cut myself. And he ended up saying, "It took me about $7,000 to make a jig to do that", and about two weeks later he gave me a guitar with the controls on the bottom.

'I look at the Stratocaster like I look at the Rolls Royce. I've spent my life reading about that marvellous automobile, and how it was built, 'cause I'm a pilot, and Rolls Royce are also involved in aviation. There's nothing like the Rolls Royce in this world. And the Stratocaster is the Rolls Royce of guitars. Even though I don't know all the groups now that are playing it and using it, I do know one thing: with the Strat you can go into many different worlds where a hollow-bodied guitar won't go. So that's why I play it – I play the best. I drive the best when I drive, and I play the best when I play.'

Chicago guitarist OTIS RUSH recorded a series of classic singles for the Cobra label which became a huge influence on the British blues movement. They were all made with his first Fender Strat.
'I bought my Strat at a store on 18th and Halsted in Chicago from a guy called Maury, who used to

look after all the guys. It was Earl Hooker who turned me on to the Strat – he was the one guy in Chicago that had all the new stuff, and he'd always be coming by with all kinds of gimmicks. The musicians I knew didn't have any stuff, but Earl Hooker had everything. He was the first guy I ever saw with a guitar with two necks, he was the first guy I saw with the Bassman, too.

'Before I had that Strat I had a cheap guitar and a cheap amp, and man, when I got that guitar I could turn up loud, and it was so exciting! You could cut through the audience, with the guitar and the horns, and the sound was just great.

'Earl Hooker was where I really hear my lines from. And Robert Nighthawk, who Earl Hooker learned from, that's what Earl told me. Earl

'ALL THESE YEARS I'VE BEEN TRYING TO THINK OF ONE, BUT NOW I GOT A NAME FOR MY GUITAR. I'M GONNA TAKE IT TO MEET LUCILLE AND LUCY.'

Otis Rush

showed me how to use the slide, but me being left-handed, upside down it didn't sound the same. So I tried to play these things without the slide, and that's where my guitar style came from. Later on my Strat got stolen from the 708 Club, and I bought an Epiphone guitar from Jimmie Johnson, but for clean sounds that Strat couldn't be beat. So a couple of years ago the guys from the Fender shop built me a new one, and it's just as good as the guitar I had all those years ago, maybe a little better.

'All these years I've been trying to think of one, but now I got a name for my guitar. I'm gonna take it to meet Lucille and Lucy – and the name of my guitar is Let Me Live. Let Me Live

means the guitar does let you live. You can put it in the corner and it's waiting for you. Keep clean strings on it, look after it, and it'll look after you!' In fact I think I'll call it Let Me Live . . . Smooth!'

BUDDY GUY, one of the last great Chicago electric guitarists, helped inspire the likes of Eric Clapton to pick up a Strat.
'In the beginning I tried to make my own guitars, and then one day when I was in high school, Guitar Slim played town with a Strat, with a fish-line instead of a strap, and I thought whatever that is, I gotta have one. I moved to Chicago in 1957 and finally got one for myself, and found it was the only guitar for what I was doing – a lot of times I would make mistakes and drop it, then

'THAT GUITAR WAS THE ONE THAT GOT ME INTO CHESS, AND WHEN I LOST IT, THAT ONE HAD TO BE THE WORST PAIN – THE WAY THEY WAS MAKING THEM THEN WAS SO NICE.'

Buddy Guy: one of the first prominent Strat users in the blues field

pick it up and it was still there. Theresa Needham, who ran a club in Chicago, bought it for me, a sunburst one.

'I was in Africa on a tour for the State Department in 1969, and naturally I had my Fender guitar with me. Now we only had a small station wagon so we couldn't load it inside, and packed it on top. And due to us traveling about 90 or 100 miles an hour it flew off. I looked back and saw it bouncing around in the middle of the street, and another automobile was coming towards it. So we stopped, and I ran to lay down

in front of the guitar to keep the other car from running over it. The case had busted open, and I looked and there were scratches all over it. I'm gonna start to cry, then I picked it up, and it was still in tune, all apart from the top E which was a little flat. It still played as well as it did when I first bought it.

'I'd use that guitar with the switch in between there – they didn't make the [five-way] switch for it yet. I thought it was a great sound. That was the guitar that Eric used to try to get me to sell, but I would never sell it.

'That guitar was the one that got me into Chess, and when I lost it, that one had to be the worst pain – the way they was making them then was so nice. It was stolen when I was playing in Canada. I'd left it at home so it would be safe. I knew who stole it – I had a little dog that I used to give to a neighbor to look after, so her son knew I was away. I even tried to buy it back off him, but I never could get it back. I've lost a lot of guitars or had them stolen over the years, but that was the one that hurt most.'

HANK MARVIN owned what was probably the first Fender Stratocaster in Britain.
'The first time I actually saw a Stratocaster was on the cover of the first Crickets album, *The "Chirping" Crickets*, and Buddy Holly was holding a sunburst Strat. To see a guitar that shape in 1957 was amazing. Bruce Welch and I were in the same skiffle group in Newcastle at the time and we looked at this and thought "What on earth is that?" If I remember right you couldn't see the headstock in the photo, just the body; we were very impressed by the three pickups and the sensuous body shape, plus the shape of the pickguard – it looked very futuristic. Later on we saw a photo of Buddy Holly and the whole band working in a music paper and you could clearly see the whole guitar and the headstock. It made an impression on a young lad. That would have been in '58 or '57.

'The first Strat I actually saw in the flesh was

the one that we had sent over from Fender in the States. We couldn't get new American instruments in the UK – there was some sort of import ban. Then Cliff came to me one day and said, "I'd like to buy you a really good guitar." We all loved the sound of the Strat, the Buddy Holly sound, so that's what we decided to go for. First of all we had the brochure sent over, and we all pored over the brochure. In fact, we also liked the sound that James Burton got with Ricky Nelson and we knew he used a Fender, so we assumed that was a Strat too. We went through the brochure and found the top line model was the one with the bird's eye maple neck, the tremolo arm and the gold hardware, and that's what we got. Then later on we found James Burton was using a battered old Telecaster. But that didn't matter because we had this new Strat and the embryonic sound that I would become famous for was beginning to take place, with echo and so forth.

'It's difficult to say now what it was like seeing that Stratocaster in the flesh for the first time. It's pretty old hat now because everybody's seen so many, but at the time it was a little bit like seeing an instrument from another planet – it just didn't look like a guitar. We were so knocked out with the way it looked we hardly wanted to play it.

'The first single I used the Strat on was "Travelling Light". Coincidentally at that time I had just got hold of an echo box and a Vox amp and was starting to formulate my sound. With the Strat I was able to develop a technique where I held the tremolo in my hand and could make the note sing like a human voice. That opened up a whole world of possibilities, and became the basis for all of my style with the Shadows.

'When I saw Hendrix on *Top of the Pops* playing "Hey Joe" I thought it was sensational, even more so because he was playing a Strat and getting a great sound out of it. I felt that when I was hearing those kinds of guitar sounds that that's a direction I should have probably gone in, but we were kind of locked in a situation that was hard to get out of. You get locked or

pigeonholed and it's very hard to get out of that slot that people put you into. So I remained in my slot like a good boy.

'To see a guitar like this in '57 was amazing, but I still think it is a fantastic instrument. It's a classic, uncluttered and very simple, there's nothing that's extraneous about it – everything that's on the guitar works. It looks incredible, and I think the fact that so many people have copied it or used it as the basis for their designs even now tells us how important a design it was – but back then it was something quite sensational.'

'IT'S DIFFICULT TO SAY NOW WHAT IT WAS LIKE SEEING THAT STRATOCASTER IN THE FLESH FOR THE FIRST TIME. IT'S PRETTY OLD HAT NOW BECAUSE EVERYBODY'S SEEN SO MANY, BUT AT THE TIME IT WAS LIKE SEEING AN INSTRUMENT FROM ANOTHER PLANET.'

Hank Marvin

ROBIN TROWER rose to fame with Procol Harum. He has played Strats exclusively ever since turning to them in the late Sixties.

'Buddy Guy was the first guitarist I heard who really seemed to be getting a real vocal thing out of the Strat, back in the very early Sixties. I remember getting a Strat because of Buddy Guy and not being able to get a damn thing out of it, so I gave it up for a little while. Then in the late Sixties, I was in Procol Harum, we were on tour supporting Jethro Tull. Martin, the guitar player, had a Strat as a spare guitar and I just happened to pick it up one day at sound check and I thought, "Whoa, wait a minute." I went out and bought one the very next day and I've

---

'IT'S A VERY HARD GUITAR TO GET SOMETHING OUT OF,

BUT IT'S THE MOST REWARDING – IT REWARDS YOU FOR

THE WORK YOU PUT IN.'

Robin Trower and '62 Strat

not really played anything else since.

'I had a collection of about 14 or 15 Strats which I'd gathered over the years of being in America during the Seventies, and they were stolen in about 1980. Luckily enough I did have my two favorites with me in England at the time, but the rest of them were gone. It was heartbreaking. I vowed never to buy another vintage guitar after that. I've always stuck with buying new ones.

'I think it's the most expressive of all the electric guitars. It has the most vocal tone – it's the nearest to the human voice that you can get. You've got a great range there even when you just use one pickup, and then when you get into the in-between pickup things it's pretty limitless. It's a very hard guitar to get something out of, but it's the most rewarding – it rewards you for the work you put in. I've tried messing about with bits and pieces of it but always come back to the standard, the original sort of set up with the old bridge piece and the vintage pickups and a three-way switch. I don't get into any of this new-fangled stuff.'

Although GEORGE HARRISON grew to fame with the aid of a Gretsch Country Gent, he reckons missing out on the Stratocaster early on scarred him for life.

'If I'd had my way, the Strat would have been my first guitar. I'd seen Buddy Holly's Strat, I think on the *"Chirping" Crickets* cover, and tried to find one, but in Liverpool, in those days, the only thing I could find resembling a Strat was a Hofner Futurama. If you look through old archive photos you might find a picture of me playing one of those things. It was very difficult to play, had an action about half an inch off the fingerboard, but nevertheless it did look kind of futuristic.

'Then when I was in Hamburg I found out that some guy had a Strat for sale, and I arranged that I was going to go first thing the next morning and buy it. I believe it was a white one. And this fella, who was the guitar player in Rory Storm And The Hurricanes, the band Ringo was in, found out about it too, and he got up earlier and went and bought it. By the time I got there it had gone. I was so disappointed it scarred me for life, that experience. I think after that happened I got the Gretsch; it was a denial kind of thing.

'It was funny, 'cause all these American bands kept coming over to England, and saying, "How did you get that guitar sound?" And the more I listened to it, the more I decided I didn't like the guitar sound I had. It was crap. A Gretsch guitar and a Vox amp, and I didn't like it. But those were early days, and we were lucky to have anything when we started out. But anyway, I decided I'd get a Strat, and John decided he'd get one too. So we sent our roadie, Mal Evans, out, said go and get us two Strats. And he came back with two of them, pale blue ones. Straightaway we used them on the album we were making at the time, which was *Rubber Soul* – I played it a lot on that album, the most noticeable thing was the solo on "Nowhere Man", which John and I both played in unison.

George Harrison

'**ALL THESE AMERICAN BANDS KEPT COMING OVER TO ENGLAND, AND SAYING, "HOW DID YOU GET THAT GUITAR SOUND?" AND THE MORE I LISTENED TO IT, THE MORE I DECIDED I DIDN'T LIKE THE GUITAR SOUND I HAD. IT WAS CRAP.**'

'Later, I think in 1967 judging by the color scheme, I decided to paint it. In that period every-thing was more colorful, colorful clothes, colorful

houses and cars, and it was just logical to have a colored guitar. So I got some Day-glo paint out of a tin and just painted it with a brush. And it's not so much a great paint job, but that's the way it came out – there's some of Patti Boyd's nail var-nish on the top, green glittery stuff. And the gui-tar's called Rocky. I've used it for years, right through from 1969 or 1970. Now I've got one of the George Formby models [*Eric Clapton – ed*] which has the boosted pickups, and I use that quite a lot now.

'I don't have a whole lot of Strats. I've got a sunburst one, one that Eric gave me quite a few years ago. There was one that was stripped to the wood that I gave to Spike Milligan. He was at my house one day with Peter Sellers – Peter was play-ing the drums, Spike was playing the piano, and I was playing guitar. Then Spike got off the piano and wanted to play the guitar, so I plugged him in to this Strat through a little Champ amplifier. He said, "Oh, I haven't played for 30 years", but he

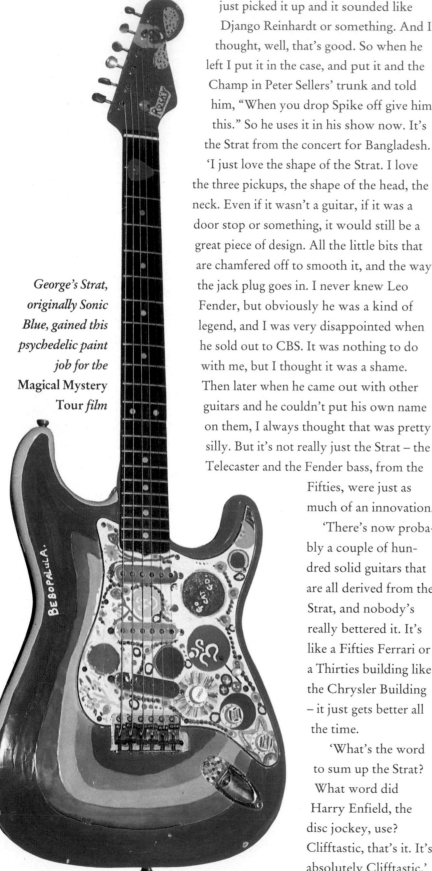

George's Strat, originally Sonic Blue, gained this psychedelic paint job for the **Magical Mystery Tour** *film*

just picked it up and it sounded like Django Reinhardt or something. And I thought, well, that's good. So when he left I put it in the case, and put it and the Champ in Peter Sellers' trunk and told him, "When you drop Spike off give him this." So he uses it in his show now. It's the Strat from the concert for Bangladesh.

'I just love the shape of the Strat. I love the three pickups, the shape of the head, the neck. Even if it wasn't a guitar, if it was a door stop or something, it would still be a great piece of design. All the little bits that are chamfered off to smooth it, and the way the jack plug goes in. I never knew Leo Fender, but obviously he was a kind of legend, and I was very disappointed when he sold out to CBS. It was nothing to do with me, but I thought it was a shame. Then later when he came out with other guitars and he couldn't put his own name on them, I always thought that was pretty silly. But it's not really just the Strat – the Telecaster and the Fender bass, from the Fifties, were just as much of an innovation.

'There's now probably a couple of hundred solid guitars that are all derived from the Strat, and nobody's really bettered it. It's like a Fifties Ferrari or a Thirties building like the Chrysler Building – it just gets better all the time.

'What's the word to sum up the Strat? What word did Harry Enfield, the disc jockey, use? Clifftastic, that's it. It's absolutely Clifftastic.'

ERIC CLAPTON and 'Blackie' have become one of the most successful partnerships in rock music. Although Blackie has now been retired, Eric's favorite Strat lives on in the shape of his own signature model, Blackie 2.

'The first guitar I ever saw was on TV. Jerry Lee Lewis was doing "Great Balls Of Fire". And that just threw me – it was like seeing someone from outer space. And I suddenly realized that here I was in this village that was never going to change, yet there on TV was something out of the future. And I wanted to go there! Actually he didn't have a guitarist, but he had a bass player, playing a Fender Precision Bass, and I said, "That's a guitar." I didn't know it was a bass guitar, I just knew it was a guitar, and again I thought, "That's the future – that's what I want." After that I started to build one, tried to carve a Stratocaster out of a block of wood, but I didn't know what to do when I got to the neck and the frets and things.

'I was a Gibson man throughout my early career, mainly because of Freddy King. I'd seen the cover of *Let's Hide Away And Dance Away*, where he's playing a Les Paul goldtop. I went out after seeing that cover and scoured the guitar shops and bought one. That was my guitar from then on, and it sounded like Freddy King.

'The story of how I got my first Stratocaster comes from when I was in Nashville in 1970 with Derek and the Dominoes, and I went into this shop called Sho-Bud. In the back they had a rack of Stratocasters and Telecasters, all going for $100 each. No one was playing them then, 'cause everybody was going for Gibsons – Les Paul models were ruling the roost for guitar heroes! But Steve Winwood had got me interested in them, because he was playing a blonde-neck Strat. It sounded great. Then I thought, "Well yeah, Buddy Guy used to play one", and I thought of Johnny Guitar Watson playing one on the *Gangster Of Love* album. So I just bought a handful of them and brought them all back to England. I gave one to George Harrison, one to Steve Winwood, and another to Pete Townshend.

'I'VE MOVED AROUND WITH GUITARS AND TRIED MANY DIFFERENT THINGS, AND I'VE ALWAYS COME BACK TO THE STRATOCASTER.'

Eric Clapton playing Blackie 2, now available as a production signature model

I kept three, and out of them I made one – Blackie. I just took the body from one, the neck from another, and so on. I have no idea what year the various parts are, so it's not a good collector's guitar at all. Well, it is now!

'That guitar has been with me through all kinds of scrapes. I remember in Jamaica, rehearsing the band I had for *461 Ocean Boulevard*, in the middle of the night in this cinema we'd rented. We could only get to play in it in the night, from 12 o'clock to 6 o'clock in the morning. I remember ending a Chuck Berry number by accidentally falling over. That was the cue for the drum beat to end the song, and I crushed some parts of my Blackie guitar underneath me. And within half an hour it was playing as good as new, just with a few little running repairs. The body and the neck and everything else were totally gone, and I thought: this guitar is my life! It can take as much damage as me! And I've never felt quite that secure with any other guitar. I can pick it up, drop it or bounce it off the wall and it will still be in tune and still play with heart and soul. It's irreplaceable. I remember one time I was recording when Stephen Bishop, who was playing with me, went back in the studio to add some electric guitar. He picked up my special guitar and began playing it – very brutally. This felt, to me, as if someone had taken a dagger and plunged it in my arm and was twisting it. I screamed and ran into the studio and grabbed it off him. Really, it was that bad, a physical feeling, painful. I believe that guitar has got some of me in it. So to see someone else pick it up and abuse it was unbearable.

'I've retired Blackie now – it's still a highly playable guitar, but it's just on the edge of being unplayable. I have it at home, and I play it every now and then, but it's too precious for me to take out for fear of loss or breakage or something like that. The only thing that bothers me about it is that the frets are too wide, because of the wood

The original Blackie, assembled from a group of old Strats, a well-used and well-loved guitar

being worn down. And I'm not in the mood to do anything about that – I'd rather keep it in the shape it's in. Then Fender came to me and said they'd be very interested in putting out a guitar with my name on it, and would I specify the way I wanted it.

'So in actual fact, I could have designed anything. If it had been someone else they asked it would probably not have been a Stratocaster, it would have been some new shape. But when they asked me what my favorite guitar was I said Blackie was it. I just wanted one little thing changing to fatten the sound up, so you'd have the Stratocaster sound throughout but you could fatten it up with just a tone knob. But if they could copy Blackie I wouldn't want any changes. And that was the point – it couldn't really be improved upon. I feel that guitar is now part of me.'

One of the most celebrated guitarists to come out of the British blues boom, and a valued Fender endorsee, JEFF BECK has two loves in life: old cars and old guitars.

'It was a quest to see the first Stratocaster in the flesh. I saw the first one in a film, I think it was *The Girl Can't Help It*, and all we wanted to do was to see and touch a real one and it was a long time coming. I think the first one came over in about '59 and then there were maybe three Strats and one Tele in the whole country. They were probably the most looked-at instruments in the whole of London – there were people's noses pressed to the window for three weeks. I remember skipping off school to look around guitar shops so we could find them.

'It just seems that every so often, man comes up with a correct invention – like the wheel was a good idea, particularly to have it round. This guitar that I'm holding just seems to cover all the complete spectrum of human emotion. From down there to up there and in between you've got everything you can shake a stick at. This tremolo here enables you to do anything. You can hit any note known to mankind with this. It's not like a

preset fret to fret or a manual bend, you can manual bend as well, you can do anything you want with it – a great idea. Whether it was intended to be like that, I don't know, but they used it a lot more sparingly in the Fifties when it first came out than I do now anyway. I mean, I write whole tunes with this arm!

Jeff Beck

'MY FIRST WIFE SAID, "IT'S EITHER THAT GUITAR OR ME", YOU KNOW – AND I GIVE YOU THREE GUESSES WHICH ONE WENT.'

'Every time I stare at it I think this is just a piece of wood with some wire strings on it that got me into lots of trouble, and yet I look around me and it must have got me all the material things that I needed and worked for. And it's caused a lot of trouble, all kinds of divorces and things, because my first wife said, my only wife said that, "It's either that guitar or me", you know – and I give you three guesses which one went.

'The ultimate sounds known in the 20th century were made on one of these, so who wants to try and improve it? I suppose nothing is as constant as

Rory Gallagher

change, so it will happen, somebody will come up with something, but I'm quite happy with this. I would be happy if someone said, "Look, every-thing's burnt. God burnt all the guitars and just left you that one." I'd still put up with the creak-ing and the out-of-tuneness about it because that's what I grew up with.

'From what I understood of Jimi Hendrix it was like another arm to him – he didn't really wanna be too many places without it. There was a documentary where Chas Chandler said he even took it to the toilet with him, and I'm not quite that bad yet – I park mine outside. I'm not devoted in the way that Jimi or Stevie Ray Vaughan are – I'm just a weekend hippy as far as that goes. Although I wouldn't like to swap what I do for anything else, I don't feel this urge to jump up and play every time I see a band playing like they did, you know, which is great. I'm glad there's people like that with the guts to do it, but I'm not that in love with music in general. I sort of take it out of the air and use it and then put it back again, but they take it out of the air at the age of 12 and never put it back. Perhaps I just had too many knocks and too many bangs along the way to be in love with it the way they are. Or were.

'With the Telecaster you've got a very, very dangerous thing, because you have to be able to play. With this guitar you can bullshit your way out of anything. It's a great feeling when you've got all your stuff together and you've rehearsed properly and you know that you're gonna kill, you feel like you can, you can just destroy a whole audience with this. It's like you're gonna go into battle and you've got your gun – and that's it, except there's no bullets. Get Nigel to put some bullets in the back.'

Donegal-born RORY GALLAGHER and his battered Strat have been synonymous since his musical apprenticeship in the blues-rock outfit Taste in 1965. After 30 years together he and his Strat are indeed best friends.
'I saw this guitar in Cork City in Ireland in 1962

in the one and only music shop that was there at the time, Michael Crawley's. I was a huge Buddy Holly fan, and a Hank Marvin fan as well, of course. He showed this guitar to me, and said, "Do you wanna buy it?" Luckily, bit by bit we got it paid off, week by week, gig by gig and I've had it ever since.

'It was a sunburst Strat that it turned out someone had traded in for a red one. It's dated November '61, and in certain people's point of view this is where they hit the peak. Certain people say that '54 or '55 is the best, but the '61 is a pretty good point really. I like maple necks, like on the earlier guitars. They're probably a bit more crisp, but there's a warmth to this, a mellowness 'cause of the rosewood neck.

'This is the best, it's my life, this is my best friend. It's almost like knowing its weak spots are strong spots. I don't like to get sentimental about these things, but when you spend 30 years of your life with the same instrument it's like a walking memory bank of your life there in your arms.

'One of the most worrying times was when the guitar got stolen. I'd borrowed a new Tele off a friend which I left with the Strat. While we were away someone put a brick through the window and made off with the two of them. For a while I really felt the loss; I had to play on an old Burns and was starting to get desperate. Then I got a phone call and they'd had the guitar on television, on *Police Five*, or *Gardia Patrol* as we call it in Ireland. The guitar had been found behind a garden wall in Dublin, all scuffed up and chipped. I've cherished it ever since. I love it – how would you define that?

'The only adjustments I've done to this guitar is to put on heavier frets than normal and I've muted one tone control so it's just like a Telecaster, with an overall master tone and volume, which is important, particularly for slide, because sometimes you have to mellow down a slide sound if you're doing a Muddy Waters type of thing. Otherwise I stay as close to the original

'I GOT A PHONE CALL AND THEY'D HAD THE GUITAR ON TELEVISION, ON *POLICE FIVE*. IT HAD BEEN FOUND BEHIND A GARDEN WALL IN DUBLIN.'

as possible. The machine heads have been changed a million times, except this odd man out here, I left this sixth one out for the gypsies. It fell one night and the back came out of it, so I just left it there. It was a little bit spooky so I left it alone. It's a superstitious thing.

'People look at my guitar and think that I must treat it badly. I admit I used to throw it about a bit in the early days, but it's really just that I use it so much that over the years the paint has gone, one little chip at a time. I don't see guitars as things to be left in glass cases. I love all great guitars, but they have to be used and I can get a kick out of a $15 Silvertone too. It's not meanness, it's just that any guitar over x-hundred dollars just becomes a status symbol. Then again, I grew up in a time when I remember Telecasters and Strats being about $250 to $350, whatever.

'I hate using your one-line clichés, but this guitar is part of my psychic make-up. I've had troubles with it but I'm fortunate enough. It's like B.B. King has a hundred Lucilles, I've only got one Strat. I don't even call it a woman's name or whatever. It's just, from where I came from, to own a Stratocaster was like monumental – it was impossible. They got me posing in front of Michael Caine's house with it so it can't be all that bad!

'There'll be arch battles for as long as we go on about the warmth of Les Paul guitars and the twang of a Telecaster and all that, but I would panic before I go on stage without this guitar – it would have to be a Strat, and this one in particular.'

JEFF LYNNE has enjoyed seemingly countless hits with his own outfits, while as a producer he's worked with everybody who's anybody.

'In the early Sixties you'd go around the guitar shops in Birmingham and the best one in the shop was always the Fender Stratocaster. It was like a big spaceship thing, compared with the others. And I always wanted to get that one down and play it, but this guy would always come along and go, "Get your hands off – play one of these", meaning one of the cheap and nasty ones. So that was a big thing in wanting one, that it was so taboo to pick it off the wall. Then when I did finally get one off the wall it was absolutely marvellous.

'It was just a magnificent design and it still is, really. The more people mess with the shape, the worse it looks. The Stratocaster's definitely a modern work of art. Even though there's millions of them and they're mass-produced, it's just a fantastic piece of work. And just to look at one – it's better than a painting to me.'

Jeff Lynne

TONY JOE WHITE:

'Tina Turner had heard of one song that my wife and I had written called "Undercover Agent For The Blues", and she wanted me to come over to New York and play guitar on the session. She said "I want your guitar to sound just like it did on the demo, nothing changed," So I brought up my old Super Reverb amp to New York and my beaten up old '58 Strat. She was standing there looking at it and just laughing, and she was going, "God, I haven't seen stuff like that since the old Mississippi days." Then I plugged it in, and she kinda quit laughing and started getting into it!'

Swamp rock king Tony Joe White gets back to basics with an old Strat and Fender Bassman

'THE STRATOCASTER'S DEFINITELY A MODERN WORK OF ART …

JUST TO LOOK AT ONE – IT'S BETTER THAN A PAINTING TO ME.'

HOTEI:

'When I got a Stratocaster for the first time, I was 15 or 16. I was actually more crazy about rock 'n' roll music in general than the guitar. To tell the truth, I actually couldn't control it very well at the

*Hotei, Japan's most popular
home-grown guitarist*

beginning. Then I tried harder and harder to get into it, and finally realized it was on my side. I think the Stratocaster sounds very natural. It expresses your feelings or emotions directly – when you are sad it sounds sad, and when you are angry it sounds angry.'

ROY ROGERS:

'I worked my way through Fenders. My first guitar was a Fender Duo-Sonic, then I had a Tele for a long time, then I worked my way up to a Strat. I got it about eight years ago and it's been part of my show ever since. It's versatile, especially for slide guitar, which is my style of playing. The contoured body is so comfortable to play, it's got a nice wide neck. It's just real conducive to helping you say whatever you want to say.'

SHERMAN ROBERTSON:

'The first time I saw a Stratocaster was when I went to see Ike and Tina Turner play, about '65. Ike was playing a sunburst Stratocaster. It sounded really nice and crisp – at the time everybody was using Gibsons, for that sound and sustain. I think overall the Stratocaster is a more versatile guitar, because of the different sounds you can get. You can play lead, you can play a little rock 'n' roll on it. You get a real good clean sound out of it, and to me, if you get the sound clean, with nothing covered up – that's the sound I like.'

Sherman Robertson

Best-known for his partnership with a battered old Telecaster, KEITH RICHARDS, who inducted Leo Fender into the Rock And Roll Hall Of Fame, is also one of the world's biggest Stratocaster fans.

Keith Richards

'THIS IS LIKE PICKING UP A STRADIVARIUS AND SAYING, "OKAY, NOW I'M IN THE BIG LEAGUE." THIS IS THE BIG BOY'S TOOL, YOU KNOW. THIS IS NO TOY. THIS IS THE HARDWARE DEPARTMENT.'

'It's like guns, you know. The Telecaster is like a Sten gun – very accurate at short range. But with the Strat you've got a far wider range of tone and feel – it was just the perfect next step in the range of guitars.

'Leo perfected the Telecaster. When I first heard James Burton play with Ricky Nelson in the mid Fifties I thought, that guitar is an amazing piece of work, let alone the player. When you hit the Tele right, it's got a spin on it, it's got a sound you cannot duplicate. They make copies, but the original has got that little bit of grit in there, and really nobody knows how Leo did this. It's like Leo Fender, Leonardo Da Vinci. Leo's an artist, an original. Everything that comes out of Japan is a copy of the Strat or the Tele, because it's the perfect shape. It's all part of God's creation and that's why we play them. They're the best guitars in the bloody world.

'I've got a couple of Strats. I've got a '57 that I stole off Ronnie Wood – well, I talked it out of him, and it's a beauty. It's been painted white, but that doesn't matter – you can soon wear the paint off. And the other thing is with these guitars you can look at the fingerboards and you can see who's been playing them before and how they played – it's almost like a graph. Some of 'em are burnt all up here, or some are burnt down here, so you can say, "Oh, he played rhythm", you know? You can read the history just by looking at the neck. You see how the frets are worn down and you know they've been in one person's hands for a long time. And then you know it's a good guitar.

'When Leo made the electric guitar he didn't stop there. Not only did he make the best electric guitars from the very beginning, but, smarter than that, he made the amplifier to go with it. You can make the best electric guitar in the world, but if it's put through the wrong amplifier you're not going to get the best out of it. And the fact is that for 20 years now I've used a Fender Twin with a Telecaster or a Stratocaster. If I really want to get down to business then they match, boom, like a matched pair. You know, when I inducted Leo into the Rock And Roll Hall Of Fame I thought it was slightly ridiculous. I mean, he brought me in – it shouldn't have been me inducting Leo, it should have been Leo inducting me, 'cause that's what happened. But since he couldn't be there. . .

'When you've got six or seven pounds of guitar hanging from your shoulder and you've got to move, if it's not balanced right, if it's too heavy, you're working against the grain. But with Leo's stuff, the Tele, the Strat or even the Precision Bass, when it's around your neck you're not aware you're carrying weight. It's there to play and you don't worry about it. It doesn't drag you down, it doesn't put your back out. It's perfection. And you can adjust it, anything on here can be flavoured if it's not right. And the neck. . . I feel like I'm trying to sell them to you. Buy a Fender. You can't go wrong.

'I started out on semi-acoustic guitars and then went to Gibsons. Gibson make good stuff but they're heavy. When you've got to stand up with them for a few hours, especially the best ones, there's too much weight on them and your hands start to drag and you're not playing as well. And I think it was around the late Sixties or early Seventies that I finally found my first Telecaster and then my first Strat, and that's when I realized I'd graduated. That I could actually handle the thing. Because unless you can play it well you'll always have James Burton and a host of other players in the back of your mind. This is like picking up a Stradivarius and saying, "Okay, now I'm in the big league." This is the big boy's tool, you know. This is no toy. This is the hardware department.

'The other great thing is that you can insert the latest pickup into them, and it's no problem. When you open them up, especially the Telecasters, they were all wired by these chicks and you have either a Mary, a Virginia or a Gloria. I've got two Marys and a Gloria. And these chicks are all still around. You kind of fall in love with them as well as the guitar. You wonder what Mary looked like, and you get all romantic about it.

'What epitomizes a Stratocaster? It's like saying explain a Stradivarius to me. Books have been written about it. In a way all of this is an exercise in futility, because the proof is here in the guitar,

this is it. The touch, the feel, the elegance. It can take hard knocks and you know it'll function perfectly when you need it next. It's as sturdy and strong as a mule, yet it has the elegance of a racehorse. It's got everything you need, and that's rare to find in anything. In people, in animals, in life, you know. The man made a work of art here. This is the Stradivarius.'

BONNIE RAITT has become one of the most highly regarded slide guitarists of the Eighties and Nineties – and all with the aid of an old Fender bought for $120.

'HOW DO I EXPLAIN THE APPEAL OF THIS GUITAR? IT'S SORT OF LIKE HOW YOU PICK A PERSON THAT YOU WANNA HANG OUT WITH – IT JUST FITS.'

'I got my first Strat in 1969 when I was 19 years old. This is it, and I've used it at every gig ever since. I picked it up at about 3 o'clock in the morning – a friend of mine tipped me onto it for $120. That was what got me, plus I'd seen a lot of my heroes playing 'em and I figured it was a good place to start. At that point I was still a kind of a folk musician and playing acoustics, but a lot of the blues men that I really liked, like Mississippi Fred McDowell, Lightnin' Hopkins and Muddy Waters, played electric to be able to cut through and get out to the audience in small clubs. A lot of people don't shut up unless you have an electric guitar!

'How do I explain the appeal of this guitar? It's sort of like how you pick a person that you wanna hang out with – it just fits. On this particular guitar these are Strat pickups, which are probably from around '65 which is when the guitar is from. This is a different neck from the one it came with

Bonnie Raitt

nobody made a better guitar than a Stratocaster, and nobody ever will. But this guitar is like a record of every gig, recorded in every knock on the wood. A couple of years ago Fender made an exact replica of this guitar for me – they used a micrometer on it! So that gave me a couple of alternatives to use, though they aren't gonna ever sound the same as this one 'cause this one's so old. There's something about the soul of a guitar as it lives with you and you play a lot of gigs on it, you know. Experience counts with music – this one's got experience.

'I'm sure that one of the reasons everybody wants to talk about the Strat is because we all love the shape and we love the design. You don't need to improve on a perfect thing and there's something about this shape that is at once masculine and feminine. It really fits everybody's body that wears it. I guess it will go down in history as one of the great designs. Then the Strat has just a unique combination of pickup sounds – I just love the way it sounds and I'm glad that Leo Fender was born, basically.

'I don't collect guitars – I buy 'em as I need 'em. I think they should be played. I think people that have beautiful guitars or cars or anything else and let 'em sit in the garage and warehouse . . . that is sort of like stockpiling wives. They are supposed to be played – this is a tree, honor it, play it, let the music live, don't put it in a storehouse some place in Tokyo and say look what I got, show it at parties. That's not what this is about.

'When you think about the combined musical contribution of everybody that's played Fender guitars, it's just mind-boggling. There'd be no rock 'n' roll, there would be no rhythm and blues without Leo's contribution. The tone is everything. Right after the inspiration and the talent, you know, that interaction between how the instrument speaks back to you and how you speak through it, is the perfect extension of a human being – an extension of your hands and your heart and your groin and your soul. It's a perfect match. Leo, wherever you are, [kiss] thanks a lot.'

originally – it's been on ever since I've had it. Somebody changed it – it's thinner, it fits my hands better.

'Hendrix and Eric Clapton were the people that really impressed me with the tone of this guitar, and since then Lowell George and Ry Cooder and a lot of other people who I admire have always played Strats. They are really consistent so I know that if I ever lost this I could replace it and still have something that sounded good, 'cause

As guitarist with Neil Young, Bruce Springsteen and others, NILS LOFGREN has garnered great respect as a guitarist, not least for his ability to play and bounce on a trampoline at the same time.

'You know, if I had to make suggestions to Leo Fender when he was putting the Strat together, I'm not sure I'd come up with anything he didn't. He must have got some good advice, like the way you have individual bridge parts to tune each string makes such sense to me, and the way the whole thing's put together and the way the volume's so close to hand.

'When I play live, where I'm most at home, you find those moments where you want to drive down, you get very intimate, so I'll be barely touching the string. But then as things get cranking, you build in some crescendos and things get exciting and you start really wailing. Most guitars will go out of tune at this point, when you lean on the string too hard. But for some reason the Strat is rock solid. You can get real physical and manhandle it, but it's still there for you. And I like to jump back and forth between those moods, because that's what music makes me feel. With this guitar I can do that, and it doesn't have to be like some chore or effort.

'One of the nice things about working with Bruce Springsteen is that he plays a Tele, and the two complement each other real nicely. But I'll tell you a story about Bruce. One time we were in Sydney, Australia on the *Born In The USA* tour, and on our night off Neil Young was playing in the same arena. I called up Bruce, said we've got to go and see Neil, and on the night I went up to play "Tell Me Why" with Neil, which I did on the *After The Goldrush* album. At the end of the night Neil asked if Bruce would get up and play, and you know what he's like, I was telling him, "You got to do it, you got to do it", and this to me was really exciting 'cause they've both been dear friends and I love both of them and their music. And I got my Strat out for Bruce, with a Fender Super Reverb amp, and got it all set up, caught it

in between the pickups, dialed it in just the way I like it for a great sound. They go through the song, every guitar player's taking turns, and I'm

---

'THE STRAT IS ROCK SOLID. YOU CAN

GET REAL PHYSICAL AND MANHANDLE

IT, BUT IT'S STILL THERE FOR YOU.'

Nils Lofgren

Steve Miller

'I was lucky, I got turned on to the Stratocaster early. I lived in Texas and there was this store called McCord's Music that was one of the first Fender franchises, and they provided instruments for all the musicians at the Big D Jamboree. I was already playing guitar, because Les Paul had taught me to play when I was five, and I had a little Gibson. Leon Rose was the first guy who played a Stratocaster and he was on a Country show in Dallas in 1953, and as soon as I heard one, I wanted one. So I started my first band in 1956, and we went straight to Stratocasters.

'A Stratocaster has always reminded me of a sailboat. It's perfect in design – there's really nothing left to be done. When Leo Fender built this instrument he really cast the perfect shape in that, if you look at this guitar, there's really nothing that could be improved on it.

'I guess if you took all the Country and Western music there is in the world, and you took a lot of the rock 'n' roll, Jimi Hendrix, Eric Clapton and Stevie Ray Vaughan and then took away the Stratocaster, you wouldn't have much left. It's a tool that all of our favorite artists and musicians and guitarists have used from the begin-

kinda trying to nudge Bruce up to the front with Neil, and sure enough, finally he goes out, cranks the thing, and they do this incredible 10-minute dual solo to "Down By The River". And Bruce isn't known as a lead guitar player, but that night he played the greatest lead guitar I've ever heard him play, as good as anything I've ever heard. He gets a great sound on his Tele but that night there was something different going on, and there was a freedom that I've never heard in his playing. I'm prejudiced, but I think having that sound on a Strat had some part in it.'

'IF YOU TOOK ALL THE COUNTRY AND WESTERN MUSIC THERE IS IN THE WORLD, AND YOU TOOK THE ROCK 'N' ROLL, JIMI HENDRIX, ERIC CLAPTON AND STEVIE RAY VAUGHAN AND THEN TOOK AWAY THE STRATOCASTER, YOU WOULDN'T HAVE MUCH LEFT.'

ning. The Strat is the most American of things – it includes everybody. Think about it – you take the twangiest country and western guitar you ever heard, and then you take Jimi Hendrix, then you take everything in between. And this guitar has produced all of those tones. It seems to suit every style, every sound, and it's its simplicity that makes it work that way. Leo Fender was truly the Henry Ford of guitars – and maybe better than Henry Ford because no one's really improved this design since Leo.

'One of my Stratocasters is very special. I had the body, no neck on it, and it was primered without any electronics in it. And my wife and I were on our own boat cruising off west Canada when we were invited to meet an Indian carver called Henry Speck, who's the chief, and the keeper of the traditions for his tribe. And I was with him and going through all of his carving and his painting and it dawned on me that I had this guitar body with me, so I took it to Henry and said, "Can I leave this with you, and can you paint it, and I'll collect it next year when I come up?" And he did exactly that. It's an amazing guitar, it has such a spiritual strength to it. It's like a very powerful instrument. That's the way guitars are.'

MARK KNOPFLER was inspired to pick up the electric guitar by seeing Hank Marvin and his red Stratocaster. Several years later, Knopfler's own red Strat would become the basis for a string of hits starting with "Sultans Of Swing".
'I can still remember this Strat at the bottom of our road that I would look at every day on the way to and from school. I'd never been as close to one before – it was about three feet away on the other side of the glass, so that was a very exciting time for me because I'd just got a Fender catalogue. I know what a Fender catalogue smells like – it's got a very definite scent to it. If I could have eaten it I think I would have done.

'For a long time I just pestered my dad to death – it was what you would call obsessive. It actually began when there was a lad making one in the woodwork room, just a piece of wood that he was making into the body shape. He was doing all the contouring – he didn't have the neck on it – and I used to go down there and keep him company just to be able to hold the bit of wood. That's how bad it was – before that it was tennis racquets and me sister's hockey stick or anything I could get hold of that was like a guitar.

'Eventually my poor old dad relented and he got me an electric guitar, and of course it had to be *Mark Knopfler*

'I KNOW WHAT A FENDER CATALOGUE SMELLS LIKE – IT'S GOT A VERY DEFINITE SCENT TO IT.'

red, just like Hank's. He couldn't get me a Fender 'cause he couldn't afford it, so he paid £50 ($125) for this Hofner, which was like a copy but not an exact one – they weren't making exact copies then. It was different but the basic shape was there. It was a big stretch for my dad but that's what I got, and when I walked out of the shop the old guy in there said, "Stick at it!"

'I didn't have the nerve to ask my dad for an amplifier, so I made a little connection and then blew up the family radio, which didn't improve my standards at the time. I used to actually put the head of the guitar on the arm of a chair; you could put your head down on the chair and it would get louder. Even after they had gone to bed I would be there twanging away and falling asleep playing. It was great. Getting hold of my first amp was exciting apart from anything else, but it would be a long time before I got my first Strat.

'I finally got my first Strat from a shop called Kitchens in Newcastle. There was this old guy serving, and I remember my dad pointing at a big cello guitar saying, "That's a beautiful guitar", and I said, "No, no, no!" That was just before getting the first outfit together in '77. It had been stripped to the wood, I don't know what color it was originally, but I had it painted red immediately.

'When I did get my first Strat it woke me up a lot and made me change certain things. I can remember I changed "Sultans Of Swing" around – originally I played it on a National steel guitar, but it was a completely different tune. When I got the Strat itself it became that song, and that taught me that you often write a song in a particular way because of the instrument you're playing. But it's also a tremendous guitar for really heavy playing, too. You can really wring some stuff out of it when you've got them wound up through a big Marshall or something like that. I'm very attached to my Pensa Suhr guitar now because I can get an awful amount of power out of it, but the Strat is

Knopfler's early Sixties Strat –
for Mark, it has to be red

always very close to my heart, and I might very well end up going back to it for a lot of stuff. There's something about the old ones that gets to you.

'I just like playing guitar, and the relationship between me and the guitar has never changed. It's usually an acoustic guitar and a sofa – it has to be a sofa so I can fall asleep playing. With an armchair I end up on the floor. You wake up at four in the morning and go to bed feeling pretty bad, but that's how it's worked out.'

CHRIS REA and his pink Strat have been together for 20 years. As he explains, he never fails to get a buzz out of playing it.
'My father used to come home with these records called *The Fifty Guitars Of Tommy Garrett,* and apparently there was this guy in Los Angeles who used to get all the best session men together, and he used to use lots of acoustic guitars, like there would be ten acoustic rhythm guitars, and they'd do "Besame Mucho" and stuff like that. Very melodic stuff – a lot of people would say it was lift music, but I actually thought it was really good and that was the first thing I remember.

'Later on one of my sisters had this record by Cliff Richard called "A Voice In The Wilderness" and there was this really echoey guitar in the background and I thought it was magic. It did something very strange to me and it turned out to be this guy called Hank Marvin. That's my first recollection of an electric guitar.

'Then 20 years went by and I was at the house of a friend who was in a band. I was going out on a Saturday night with him and he had this Joe Walsh record on and I heard this strange guitar sound. I didn't know what he was doing, and this friend said to me, "Chris, that is a slide guitar."

'Later on I moved from Joe Walsh to Ry Cooder, trying to get information about any slide guitarist, and Ry Cooder virtually became my mentor. Ry tended to play melodies and I liked that a lot. So off I went in search of a Stratocaster and this is it. I actually wanted a sonic blue one,

like the one that Ry Cooder had, and couldn't find one anywhere, but I liked this pink one a lot and it's been with me ever since, 20 years. There's nothing like it.

'WHEN PEOPLE GO ON ABOUT THE STRATOCASTER THEY USUALLY MEAN THEIR OWN STRATOCASTER. IT'S A LITTLE BIT LIKE EVERYBODY KNOWS WHERE THE BEST INDIAN RESTAURANT IS, AND IT'S ALWAYS THE ONE THEY GO TO.'

'I find Strats better for slide because they sound very banjoey, very Western, you can donk them and there's a real bite to the sound. I find them more expressive, there's more light and shade in the tone when you're playing a solo – you can get really different types of sound out of them.

'I've tried everything to replace this guitar because it does have a lot of quirks which cause you problems. When you start playing with stage lights and big productions you get something called RF [radio frequency interference] which is the curse of the Stratocaster guitarist. When you turn up you get this buzz from the lighting rig – the famous Stratocaster buzz. It has a buzz and a hum – the hum you can get rid of by screening the guitar, but the RF buzz you can't get rid of. By the time you've got rid of the buzz it doesn't sound like a Stratocaster any more. I've had over 30 different types of guitar in my hands. People have said, here's a Stratocaster and it doesn't buzz. You play it and it doesn't buzz – but it doesn't sound like this one.

'When people go on about the Stratocaster they usually mean their own Stratocaster. It's a little bit like everybody knows where the best Indian restaurant is, and it's always the one they go to.

Chris Rea (opposite),
Strat, and bottleneck

Stratocasters all sound different, and everybody likes their own. They become very emotional to you. I couldn't do anything to this guitar because I don't own another Stratocaster that sounds like this one.

'I do believe we only part with a Stratocaster we're happy with when it actually wears away, like Eric Clapton's black Strat. Well, I've been playing as long as he has and that hasn't happened to me yet, but we've had to replace the top frets because I actually developed a style of playing where I would knock the slide against the neck. I used to use brass bottlenecks but now I've started to use glass ones because I've been told that this guitar will only take another two re-frets. So it's become even more precious to me. It's paid my mortgage, my gas bills – it's done everything for me.'

NILE RODGERS, founder member of Seventies disco exponents Chic, also has a reputation as one of the finest rhythm guitarists in the world, while his myriad production credits include work with the likes of Eric Clapton, Stevie Ray Vaughan and David Bowie.
'I think the first time I saw a Stratocaster was with the Beach Boys. And I didn't know what it was called, but I knew the shape and the design. When you're a kid the more pickups and knobs and switches a guitar has, the more you think you can do. So I just thought, "Oh, man – cool. What's this thing?"

'Years later I was on the road with a band called New York City, we had a hit record called "I'm Doing Fine Now" – it was about '74 and we were doing this one gig in Miami Beach. We had to lend the house band our amplifiers, so we set up all the gear and the house band used it. And the kid who played guitar in the house band played on my amplifier with a Stratocaster, and it just sounded unbelievable. And Bernard

Edwards, who was musical director of my band, said, "I told you to buy a Strat. I told you!" Then the very next day I took this big jazz guitar I had – maybe it was a Gibson Barney Kessel or something – down to the pawnshop, 'cause everybody knows that a Stratocaster is very affordable. So I traded in my Barney Kessel, I got maybe $200 or $300 back, and I got a

---

'I HAVE PROBABLY PLAYED ON AT LEAST 30 BIG RECORDS WITH THIS GUITAR. THEN I SWITCHED, AND FOR ABOUT THREE YEARS I DIDN'T GET A GOLD RECORD'

Stratocaster. And I just thought, "Man, this is a great guitar." And I took the Stratocaster back and locked myself in the bathroom in the hotel and for two days all I did was play rhythm, jigajig, jig, jig, and got it down, and then I emerged – this new transformed guy. And I've never put my Strat down since.

'I've seen the great guitar players – Buddy Guy, Hendrix, Clapton using Strats – but my own little statement about this instrument is that this one guitar right here has been on more hit records than I can imagine. I have probably played on at least 30 big records with this guitar. Then one day a few years ago I put it away and made some sort of irrational rock 'n' roll decision that I would switch to a Telecaster. So I switched guitars, and for about three years I didn't get a gold record. Then Steve Winwood called me up to play on "Higher Love", and I was just about to walk out of the house with the Tele, when I went "Mmm" and went back and got this baby. Now "Higher Love" was a pretty big record so there must be some sort of magic or karma in this thing. And now that I've picked it up again I don't think I want to put it down, ever.'

Canadian rocker BRYAN ADAMS wrote hit songs for the likes of Bachman-Turner Overdrive, Kiss and Bonnie Tyler before racking them up under his own name. The majority of those hits were written on a Fender Strat.

'There's about four songs in my band's set where I don't play a guitar – and it's incredibly humiliating. You see, a guitar is a great shelter. It's something you can hide behind. You stand there with a guitar and it's fine. But if you're standing there without anything, just a microphone, it's even more humiliating. That's why a guitar's a man's best friend.

'I'D GO TO SCHOOL IN THE DAYTIME AND I'D WASH THE DISHES IN THE EVENING, AND I DID THAT FOR A WHOLE YEAR UNTIL I EARNED ENOUGH MONEY TO BUY A FENDER STRATOCASTER.'

'I worked for a year as a dishwasher in a place in North Vancouver called the Tomahawk Barbecue – a real greasy hamburger place. I'd go to school in the daytime and I'd wash the dishes in the evening, and I did that for a whole year until I earned enough money to buy a Fender Stratocaster – a real Fender Stratocaster. As soon as I had enough money I quit the job, took the bus to the music store and bought this Fender Stratocaster which I still have today. It was white – it's now yellow – it's a '75 and it's chipped and cracked and it's got holes in it, saw marks and everything else, but it was my first Strat and I still have it. I still play it – I even drag it out on stage occasionally.

'What started me playing guitar was the Beatles, but it was Ritchie Blackmore that first fired me up about Stratocasters. I think it was

actually listening to his album *Machine Head*. We must have checked those photographs from that album out for hours, you know. We'd sit there and look at it – "Wow! It looks like a Vox amp", you know. We were really into that and I was really into his playing and to this day I still couldn't play a Ritchie riff if I had to because it's beyond me! But he's still is one of my favorite Strat players – his guitar work is fantastic.

'There's a story actually where Keith – our guitarist – and I were both at a Deep Purple concert. Keith elbowed his way to the front and as Ritchie was bending down to put a guitar in the audience, Keith grabbed it and pulled it into the audience. Ritchie just walked away and some big huge monster bouncer jumped in and pulled it away from everybody 'cause by that time everybody was having a piece of that guitar. We were both big fans of his style.

'Personally, I'm just glad Leo Fender sat down one day and sorted out the Strat, because it changed the face of music. I don't know if I can summarize my feelings towards the Strat other than by saying that in 100 years those pre-CBS guitars will be the Stradivarius of our time. There really isn't a guitar that has single-handedly influenced music as much as this guitar has. Gee, what can I tell you? Slim neck, contour body, five springs, feels like a woman, looks like a lady. I wonder if there's some sort of subliminal Leo Fender message, you know, because she feels like a woman.'

DWEEZIL ZAPPA inherited one of the world's most famous Strats, one used by his father, and by Jimi Hendrix at the Monterey Pop Festival.

'As far as Strats go, I would say I have a couple of the coolest ones around. This one is top of the list: it's the one Jimi Hendrix played at Monterey and then it was given to my dad who played it for a number of years, with different pickups and a different neck – of course, the neck was destroyed in the fire. Now it's passed onto the third generation – it's my guitar.

Bryan Adams

'A LOT OF THE STUFF THAT LEO DESIGNED GOT CHANGED OVER THE YEARS, SO NOW PEOPLE ARE SCRATCHING THEIR HEADS GOING, "WAIT A SECOND, WHY DID WE EVER CHANGE THAT – IT WAS SO MUCH BETTER BACK THEN".'

Dweezil Zappa

'I actually found the guitar at our house under a staircase, and I thought, "Oh my God, it's the Hendrix guitar, it's been left to die!" I asked my dad if I could have it rebuilt and that's what happened. He gave it to me, and the guys at Fender's Custom Shop put it together. Now it's the kind of thing that I just can't take anywhere because someone might want to steal it.

'When I was young, most of the time my dad would be playing his SG, so I really associated the Strat with Jimi Hendrix. Anything Hendrix did on the Strat was amazing – one of my favorite solos

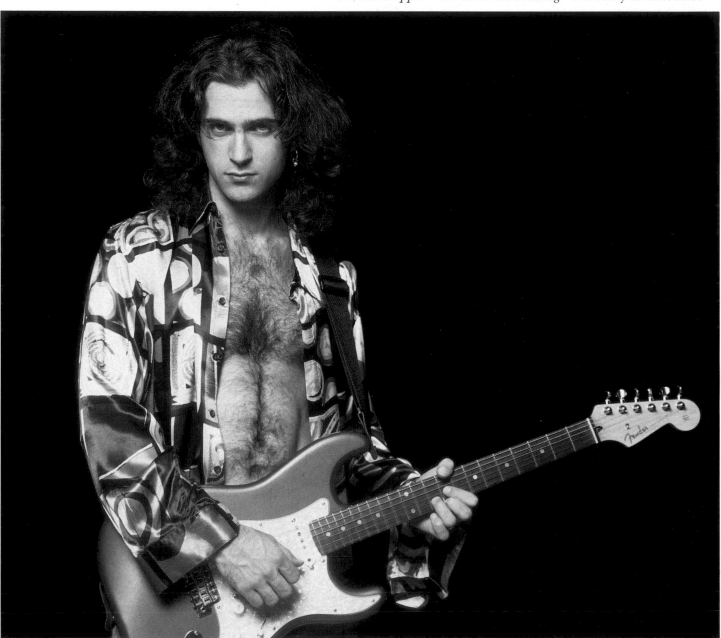

of his is "All Along The Watchtower", that's got a very specific Strat sound which I dig. My dad worked with guitar tones that were way ahead of their time. He had guitars built with weird electronics, then he got great clean sounds, then there's stuff like a song called "Watermelon In Easter Hay" that's got an amazing solo. I think he played that on the Hendrix Strat when it was in his possession and now it's mine, thank you.

'You know, I don't know a lot about Leo Fender other than he designed a whole bunch of great guitars and he was way ahead of his time. I mean a lot of the stuff that he designed got changed over the years and now people are scratching their heads going, "Wait a second, why did we ever change that – it was so much better back then." The original sounds are still the sounds that people are looking for.'

Bon Jovi's RICHIE SAMBORA turned to Stratocasters late in life; the move brought immediate results.
'Eric Clapton always epitomized the Strat for me. Anything off the *Layla* album would be a quintessential Strat sound – Eric really commanded the instrument and made me want to play guitar. After listening to that record I immediately wanted to buy an electric guitar, to go out and learn how to command the instrument and wrench the emotion out of it – that probably spurred me on to become a successful musician in my own right.

'I really started playing Strat after our second record. I was playing Gibsons, a Les Paul and an Explorer and we got all our equipment stolen – I took that as a sign from God to switch to Fender and Stratocaster. That was when I made the switch, and that was when we had our big record, *Slippery When Wet*, and everything kind of blew through the roof. So I think I took God's heed very effectively.

'The Stratocaster is probably one of the most versatile instruments ever. Leo truly created something that was very special; it has a wide range of sounds and it's very distinctive in each particular sound that it has – it's always just been a true guitar and very versatile for any music form that you can possibly play. It's probably the quintessential rock 'n' roll guitar, alongside the Les Paul Standard and Les Paul Custom and stuff that Les Paul invented. But they are two totally different instruments – I think that the Stratocaster probably has a bit more dexterity in sound and transcends different genres. You can use it in blues and jazz and rock 'n' roll and stuff like that. Leo definitely stumbled onto something that gave me a reason to have my gig and so did Lester, so I'm sure that when those two guys got together they had a lot to talk about. Les Paul and I are somehow really good friends, despite the years of difference in our ages. We often talk about Leo and Lester's relationship, and I think they both were friends and they both probably talked about their different inventions and how they changed it and how they marketed it.

'All the Strats that I own are either pre-CBS or were made when the new regime came into Fender after CBS. I don't know what happened during the CBS years. I guess that it just got less personal and there was less pride taken because a big conglomerate had taken over. It left the hands of the inventor and the guys who actually built those guitars, I think that's probably why the quality went down in the CBS years.

'When Leo invented the Stratocaster I'm sure he had a hard time selling it first, then after musicians discovered what a great instrument and great tool it was, it finally caught on. I think he gave us all a job as rock 'n' roll musicians. This is a guitar

---

'I WAS PLAYING GIBSONS AND WE GOT ALL OUR EQUIPMENT STOLEN – I TOOK THAT AS A SIGN FROM GOD TO SWITCH TO FENDER.'

---

that has survived over four or five decades now and probably will continue endlessly. I think that young musicians throughout history will probably love and pick up the Stratocaster, and learn how to play and command the instrument and give the world great songs and great music.'

Jimmie Vaughan and friend

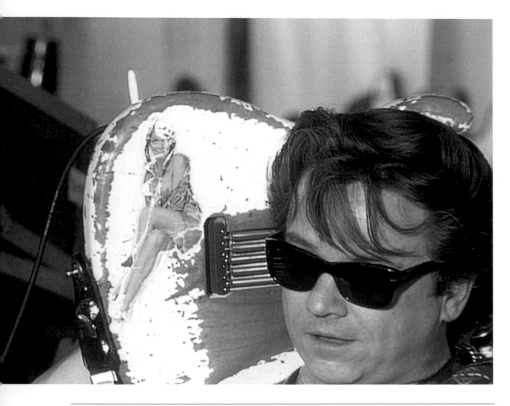

'THIS GUITAR JUST HAS ITS OWN THING. WHEN YOU PUT IT ON, IT'S LIKE PUTTING ON A PAIR OF SHOES.'

JIMMIE VAUGHAN has become one of the most respected guitarists from the Texas blues scene with his Fabulous Thunderbirds. His close musical relationship with brother Stevie Ray Vaughan even extended to sharing his Stratocaster.

'When I was about 13 or 14 I used to ride the bus down town every Saturday and go to this music store, and sit there in front of this glass case, like a gun case, which had all of the new guitars lined up: Stratocaster, Telecasters, Les Pauls and everything. And I used to stare at the Stratocaster, because it was the best-looking one. It looked like a rocket ship. "If only I had that guitar I could rule the world", was the way you felt when you looked at it. And I've never gotten over that. Now I could have any guitar I wanted, but if I go to the gig or make a record, this is the one I want.

'The Stratocaster to me is the most important guitar, because they still haven't come up with anything better. It's like . . . a '32 Ford. A '32 Ford is the main hot-rod, if you think of an American hot-rod, you think of the '32 Ford Coupe. And you can change the engine, put different wheels and different tires on, paint it different, chop the top, but it's still a '32 Ford. A Stratocaster does all the things that other guitars do. The other guitars are famous because they have a certain sound, but this one will do everything. It can be a big box Gibson sound, it'll sound like a Telecaster, it'll do everything. Plus it looks cool.

'I didn't get a Strat until about '66. I always had Telecasters before that, and Les Pauls. And I finally got one because I heard Buddy Guy. I just put this record on, it was called *Folk Festival Of The Blues*, and had Muddy Waters, Howlin' Wolf and all these guys on there – and the Stratocaster. It sounded like Buddy Guy had a brand new '57 Stratocaster with a brand new Bassman amp, and it just had that incredible sound.

'This particular guitar I bought for $150 from a friend of mine called Bill Campbell. I haven't been able to put it down since. Every year I go out and try to get a new one, or get Fender to make me a new one. I'll play it a couple of times and I always go back to this one. It's just got that special sound – it's light, and it's never let me down. I used this guitar on my new album, and on *Family Style* Stevie and I both used it. We just sort of pulled it back and forth, for all the parts. We wanted to make a record with one guitar – so this was it. I figure if you need to play acoustic or something there may be some reason to use another kind of guitar, but for my money this is it. I feel like I've been a walking Fender advertisement for 20 years. This guitar just has its own thing. When you put it on, it's like putting on a pair of shoes. In fact, the only thing that's more important, or comes anywhere close, is your shoes – if you're going anywhere. You look down at it, and you feel like you can do more than you can. That's what happens to me, anyway.'

ROBERT CRAY has become one of the most successful bluesmen of the Eighties and Nineties with the aid of his 'ugly green Strat'.
'I first got excited about Strats when seeing Philip Guy play one backing his brother Buddy Guy in the late Seventies. It had a very bright glass-like sound and he played with a lot of reverb. At that time I played a Gibson SG Standard and an ES–345, which I'd used for my first album. It had a real deep sound 'cause of the humbuckers, but it was really too much on the low end and too bright on the high end. Fortunately, the week I started looking for a Strat I ran into the guy who had to sell the green '64 Strat I now own, and instantly I fell in love. I found that I could get the sound that I heard Philip get, and it also became easier for me to adjust the tone and volume since there were fewer knobs to fiddle with while at the microphone. I believe the year was '79. I've been a Fender man ever since.

'Later on I got a '58 Strat, a sunburst with a maple neck. It's a non-tremolo that used to belong to Steve Samuels. Now I use Strats of all sorts but mainly the Signature Strat that Fender created for me. They are such versatile guitars, and so practical, too – about the only guitar I play that isn't a Strat is a steel-bodied Telecaster made by a friend of mine, James Trussart.

'The Signature Strats came about because Fender saw me playing that green Stratocaster and told me, "We wanna make a guitar for you." I said, "Great, but tell you what, I have this '58 Strat, I'd like to have a combination of that and the '64 for the neck." So they made me a prototype, about four years ago. They found some old clay and

'I'M JUST A PLAIN OL' GUY REALLY, JUST PLUG IN AND THAT'S IT!'

used that for the fret markers – it was a really nice-feeling guitar. The guitar's a non-trem, like my '58 – the strings anchor through the body. They're the regular-style pickups, the passive ones, brighter as you go to the bridge. I trade guitars back and forth as we're playing live as they go out of tune, and I play an American Standard now as well as the Signature, just for a different feel.

'As far as the switch positions go, I normally use second and fourth. Then for some solos I go up to the fifth position – and for some to the first position. The only one I don't use is the middle position. As far as amps or effects go, I use an old Super Reverb as well as the Reissue Twins. I always use them at the same volume, around half with the treble all the way up. And that's it. If I need any more volume on stage it gets turned up in the monitors. I'm just a plain ol' guy really, just plug in and that's it! I don't have a huge collection of guitars or anything. For me the sound of a Strat with a Fender amp is really all I need.'

Robert Cray

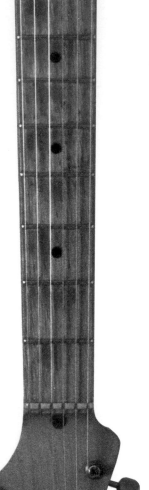

CHAPTER SEVEN

THE STRAT SOUND

The Stratocaster is probably the most recorded electric guitar ever. The following Strat-related

albums are just a small sample of the wealth of material available, but illustrate how

significantly the Strat influenced the whole course and sound of rock music.

THE FIFTIES

Although the Strat only appeared halfway through the Fifties, its influence would be felt in blues, rock 'n' roll and Leo Fender's favorite, country music.

The Fifties saw the birth of the teenager as a separate economic group with a subculture of its own. In the first half of the decade popular music had little to offer teenagers, so they turned to the cinema for their role models, in particular James Dean in *Rebel Without A Cause*. But in the middle of the decade American disc jockey Alan Freed realized just how popular the rhythm and blues records he was playing were with teenagers and coined the term 'rock 'n' roll' to describe the new music that was emerging.

The roots of rock 'n' roll were in rhythm and blues and country music, and its early exponents were Louis Jordan, Earl Bostic and Johnnie Ray.

Bill Haley: set the ball rolling

Bill Haley, although not an originator, recognized the viability of white R&B music and set the ball rolling in America with his hit from 1955, "Rock Around The Clock", as featured in the film *Blackboard Jungle*. The film sparked off cinema riots in the States, while in Britain Teddy Boys caused similar trouble. Hot on Haley's heels came Elvis Presley who in turn paved the way for Little Richard, Jerry Lee Lewis, Chuck Berry and Buddy Holly. In Britain, Elvis inspired singers such as Billy Fury and Cliff Richard, whose backing band, the Shadows, would later record on their own. Lonnie Donegan started a skiffle craze which continued into the Sixties. Skiffle made music-making accessible to many people and made the guitar a popular instrument into the bargain.

The Fender Stratocaster was brought to the attention of a great many people by Buddy Holly, who played a Strat live and in the studio. On the sleeve of his band's debut album, *The "Chirping" Crickets* (1957), Holly is shown holding a Strat, which was an integral part of their sound. Holly's development from country to rock 'n' roll can best be heard on *The Complete Buddy Holly*, especially on "Peggy Sue", where his driving rhythm guitar style is accentuated by downstrokes.

Holly's tragic early death in a plane crash in 1959, along with his contemporary Ritchie Valens, who also favored the Fender Strat, robbed rock of a major talent at the height of his powers. Unlike Valens, however, Holly left behind a considerable recording legacy to remember him by. What little we have of Valens, including the *Best of Ritchie Valens* compilation album, only hints at his capabilities. He is best known for his adaptation of the traditional song "La Bamba", as covered in the Eighties by Los Lobos who based their version on his original arrangement, and as the subject of the film *La Bamba* (1987), a bio-pic of his short career.

Gene Vincent, with his energetic and occasionally lewd stage act, represented the dangerous side of rock 'n' roll. When guitarist Cliff Gallup left Vincent's backing band, the Blue Caps, he was replaced by Johnny Meeks, a Strat player chosen for his 'treble-y, piercing sound'; indeed, Blue Caps' publicity shots of the time look like advertisements for Fender instruments. Meeks can be heard on Gene Vincent's *The EP Collection*, particularly on the tracks "Summertime" and "Dance To The Bop". Jeff Beck pays tribute to the music of Gene Vincent and his guitarists on his 1993 album *Crazy Legs*.

Some of Leo Fender's early instruments were 'test driven' by Bob Wills and his Texas Playboys. Bob Wills was a pioneer of Western Swing music, a hard-edged form of country which took in some blues and was an influence on many musicians, including Hank Williams, Chuck Berry and even Stevie Ray Vaughan. Their track "Faded Love" as included on *Anthology (1935 – 1973)* was one of Leo Fender's favorites although the guitar of Eldon Shamblin plays a purely supportive role to the song. Shamblin played a 1954 gold-painted Strat, one of the first metallic-colored instruments, and was a talented arranger and tasteful rhythm player; his jazz-tinged lead work can be heard on "Three Guitar Special" from the same album.

The best-known blues musicians who favored the Strat were Otis Rush, Buddy Guy and singer Pee Wee Crayton. Rush's best work was arguably recorded for the Cobra label in the late Fifties; it was re-issued on *Otis Rush: Double Trouble* which includes "All Your Love", perhaps his best-known song, which was covered later by John Mayall's Bluesbreakers with Eric Clapton on guitar. Although the CD sleeve shows Rush with a Gibson semi-solid guitar, Rush recalls that his Cobra work was recorded with a Fender Strat. Rush's distinctive tone and vibrato is partly due to the fact that he was a left-handed guitarist who played a right-handed guitar without restringing the instrument, as did Albert King. Still recording and touring, Rush now plays a left-handed Strat from the Fender Custom Shop but still strung for a right-handed person, thus enabling access to the higher reaches of the fretboard. Also recording in the Fifties, blues singer Pee Wee Crayton played an early Strat in the color that later became known as Dakota Red. He can be heard on the album *Wild Blues Guitarist*; as with Rush the cover illustration shows Crayton with a Gibson-type guitar!

Buddy Holly – The Complete Buddy Holly (MCA, DCDSP 807)
Ritchie Valens – Best Of Ritchie Valens (Ace, CDCHM 387)

Pee Wee Crayton

Gene Vincent – The EP Collection (See For Miles Records, SEECD 253)
Bob Wills And His Texas Playboys – Anthology (1935–1973) (Rhino, R2 70744)
Otis Rush – Double Trouble – Charly Blues Masterworks Vol 24 (Charly, CD BM 24)
Pee Wee Crayton – Wild Blues Guitarist (Import, Vivid Sound, VSCD-505)

Buddy Holly and the Crickets were probably the most visible Fender users of the Fifties

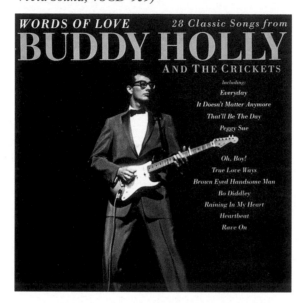

Ritchie Valens (below): his recordings only hint at his capabilities

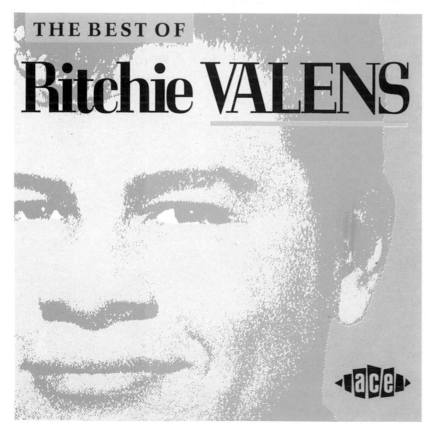

THE SIXTIES

While the Sixties was represented by a flowering of rock and guitar music, the Strat suffered from the whims of fashion in the middle of the decade as the sound of Gibson guitars dominated the British blues scene. By the end of the decade it would become apparent that as well as being appropriate for the most innocuous of surf music, the Strat could also be the vehicle for the most bombastic of guitar heroes.

With the deaths of Buddy Holly and Ritchie Valens at the end of the Fifties, Elvis drafted into the Army for military Service and Chuck Berry in prison, rock 'n' roll had lost its momentum in the States. Meanwhile in the UK, the Shadows were the precursor of a wave of British groups. Their series of instrumental hits, based around the Stratocaster guitar of Hank Marvin, inspired a number of other instrumental hits from the Ventures, Duane Eddy and Bert Weedon. Just as Lonnie Donegan had popularized the acoustic guitar in the skiffle boom, so Hank Marvin introduced the electric guitar – and the Strat – to many youngsters.

The arrival of the Beatles in 1963 changed the face of popular music forever. In contrast with many popular singers and groups of that time, the Beatles did not use session musicians or song-writers but played their own instruments and wrote their own material. The Beatles inspired the so-called Merseybeat in Liverpool and the invasion of America by a string of British bands, including the Rolling Stones, Dave Clark Five and Herman's Hermits.

In London, the Stones helped to start a British rhythm and blues boom which would produce such guitar luminaries as Eric Clapton and Peter Green (of Fleetwood Mac fame), both of whom had gained notoriety while playing in John Mayall's Blues Breakers. The focus in popular music then switched from 'swinging' London to America, where the 'flower power' movement gave rise to bands like the Doors, the Grateful

Dead and Jefferson Airplane. After achieving his first major breakthrough in the UK, American Jimi Hendrix returned to the States for a triumphant performance at Monterey. Hendrix effectively 're-invented' the electric guitar by showing the limitless sonic possibilities of the instrument, and in the process ensured the longevity of the Strat.

Along with Otis Rush and Magic Sam, Buddy Guy was part of a Chicago 'West Side sound' – urban electric blues which emphasized single-note electric guitar lead work. Arguably the most intense of these three players, Guy can be heard on the early Sixties album *The Treasure Untold*, which includes "The First Time I Met The Blues". a track with stinging lead guitar Strat work.

Like Otis Rush, Dick Dale was a left-handed guitarist who played a right-handed Strat without restringing. Dale was proclaimed the 'King of Surf Guitar', surf music largely consisting of instrumental tunes with reverb-drenched lead guitar supported by a driving drum beat and constant quavers in the bass. Dale's best work can be heard on the 1989 compilation album *King Of The Surf Guitar: The Best Of Dick Dale & His Del-Tones*, not to be confused with his long-deleted 1963 album *King Of The Surf Guitar*. An enthusiastic Strat player, Dale was one of the first guitarists to appreciate the versatility of the Strat: 'The Strat is the guitar . . . because it can be utilized to make any kind of sound.' Leo Fender originally designed a three-way pickup selector because he liked the sound of each pickup on its own, but Dale added a switch to enable the pickups to be used in combination. Although the British invasion of the mid Sixties largely overshadowed Dale's work, the influence of early Sixties surf music can still be heard today in the music of Joe Satriani.

Back in Britain, the Shadows, Cliff Richard's backing band, had a series of instrumental hits that were far less raucous and more restrained than Dale's surf music. Guitarist Hank Marvin ordered a Strat from the States after seeing one for the first time on the cover of Buddy Holly's debut album, *The "Chirping" Crickets.* Marvin's twangy lead

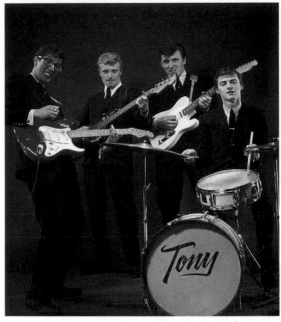

The Shadows: their publicity shots acted as unofficial Fender endorsements

guitar playing on a Strat provided a model for many of the later British electric guitarists, including Brian May, Peter Green and Gary Moore. *20 Golden Greats* features the Shadows' greatest hits including "Apache" and "FBI". Such is Marvin's strong association with the Fender Strat that he now has a signature model Strat in his name.

The electric guitar is not usually associated with soul music, and yet it has played an exceptional role in the success of Curtis Mayfield's rhythm guitar work with the Impressions. Mayfield played a Fender Strat in an unusual tuning – 'F# A# C# F# A# F#' from bottom string to top string. Using the middle pickup and plucking with his thumb, Mayfield produced a mellow tone as can be heard in the fills on "People Get Ready" from the Impressions' *Definitive Impressions*. Mayfield was a significant influence on both Jimi Hendrix and Ry Cooder.

The Beatles' guitarist George Harrison used a Strat to extend his range of sounds, as can be heard on "Nowhere Man" from *Rubber Soul*. Rather than developing a distinctive style and sound of his own, Harrison would adapt his playing to suit the song, with his Strat providing yet another dimension.

Similarly, Robbie Robertson from The Band played for the song rather than for the guitar. The

Curtis Mayfield

Band's *Music From The Big Pink* was a landmark rock album both lyrically and musically. Robertson's lean guitar-playing was executed with a Fender Strat.

The tonal possibilities of the electric guitar were largely unexploited until the arrival of Jimi Hendrix, another left-handed guitarist who played a right-handed instrument but restrung for conventional playing. The Jimi Hendrix Experience's debut album *Are You Experienced?* practically redefined the electric guitar, making feedback and distortion part of the instrument's vocabulary rather than a novelty, as can be heard in "Foxy Lady" and "Third Stone From The Sun". The Experience's second album is overall a more lyrical and melodic affair, Hendrix using the so-called out-of-phase pickup combination of bridge and middle pickups together for the chiming guitar sound of "Little Wing", "Castles Made Of Sand" and "One Rainy Wish". The five-way pickup selector didn't become a standard fitting on the Fender Stratocaster until 1977, so until then guitarists had to 'balance' the selector switch in order to obtain combinations of pickups. The Jimi Hendrix Experience's *Electric Ladyland* album was more experimental as Hendrix pushed back the musical frontiers still further. The track "Have You Ever Been (To Electric Ladyland)" shows a distinct Curtis Mayfield influence.

Buddy Guy – The Treasure Untold – Charly Blues Masterworks Vol 11 (Charly, CD BM 11)
Dick Dale – King of the Surf Guitar: The Best of Dick Dale & His Del-Tones (Rhino, RNLP 70074)

The Shadows – 20 Golden Greats (EMI, CDP 7 46243 2)
The Impressions – Definitive Impressions (Kent, CDKEND)
The Beatles – Rubber Soul (Parlophone, CDP 746 440 2)
The Band – Music From The Big Pink (Capitol, CDP 7 46069 2)
The Jimi Hendrix Experience – Are You Experienced? (Polydor, 521 036-2)
The Jimi Hendrix Experience – Axis: Bold As Love (Polydor, 847 243-2)
The Jimi Hendrix Experience – Electric Ladyland (Polydor, 847 233-3)

THE SEVENTIES

At the beginning of the Seventies the Strat was synonymous with the excesses of Hendrix and followers such as Ritchie Blackmore. But in a period which saw the height of Strat production, the guitar would also become the vehicle for more subtle exponents, such as Mark Knopfler, while Eric Clapton, who had previously done so much for the Gibson Les Paul, finally turned towards Fender's finest.

The Seventies got off to a bad start with the deaths of Jimi Hendrix, Jim Morrison and Janis Joplin. Rock proved that it was still capable of springing surprises, though, with the co-existence of heavier and louder bands which had developed out of the blues boom of the late Sixties – for example, Led Zeppelin, Black Sabbath and, the first of the heavy metal bands, Deep Purple – with glam rockers like Marc Bolan and David Bowie. Placing a high value on instrumental technique, progressive rock bands such as Genesis, King Crimson, Pink Floyd and Yes displayed an altogether more cerebral and self-conscious approach. Other technically adept musicians such as John McLaughlin combined jazz and rock into 'fusion'. In the States, so-called adult-orientated rock bands such as the Eagles and the Steve Miller Band dominated the airwaves with their sophisticated sounds. In Britain, none of these – heavy metal, progressive rock, fusion or AOR – reflected what teenagers were feeling, hence the punk explosion in 1977. Short on technical ability but long on enthusiasm, bands such as the Sex Pistols and the Clash produced some of the most exciting and highly charged music since the early days of rock 'n' roll. However, many of the punk bands were burnt out by the late Seventies, leaving the disco craze to sweep the charts. It seemed as though the electric guitar had reached its final full-stop. Then, in 1978, Eddie Van Halen updated the rock guitar vocabulary with a new set of licks and techniques on his band's debut album *Van Halen*. Here was arguably the most influential and important elec-

Joe Walsh

tric guitarist after Jimi Hendrix.

Having grown tired of the instrumental excesses of Cream in the Sixties and inspired by the example of The Band to work more closely with other musicians, in the early Seventies Eric Clapton formed Derek and the Dominoes to produce *Layla And Other Assorted Love Songs*, a classic album containing some of Clapton's best playing. Some of Clapton's guitar work with Cream could be characterized as self-indulgent, but there is no hint of it on this album. Clapton had played a Les Paul during his days with John Mayall's Bluesbreakers but changed to a Strat after hearing Buddy Guy. He can be clearly heard playing a Stratocaster on "Bell Bottom Blues", "Have You Ever Loved A Woman?" and "Layla".

With a 1961 Strat, blues rocker Rory Gallagher's album *Live In Europe* from 1972 catches the Irish blues rocker at his best. This album manages to capture the spontaneity of a Gallagher live performance. Another live album, Deep Purple's *Made In Japan* (from 1973, re-released as a three-CD set *Live In Japan* in 1993) shows the band in its classic line-up and includes "Smoke On The Water". Playing a Strat through a cranked Marshall stack, Ritchie Blackmore plucks the main riff with his fingers, a subtle but significant factor in the sound. Blackmore has claimed to be influenced as much by classical music as the work of fellow rock guitarists. Even if he wanted to, ex-Procol Harum guitarist Robin Trower

*Mark Knopfler of
Dire Straits*

could make no such claim, particularly in the 1974 album *Bridge Of Sighs*, where the influence of Hendrix can be heard.

The slick sounds of adult-orientated rock characterize the Eagles' 1976 album *Hotel California*, with Joe Walsh on a Gibson and Don Felder on a Fender giving an epic side-by-side display of virtuosity on the title track. From the same year, the Steve Miller Band's *Fly Like An Eagle* is a similarly laid-back and sophisticated album, with Miller's main guitar a Strat.

Punk guitarists generally preferred to get their thick, chunky sounds with the help of Gibsons,

Ry Cooder

and the Strat had to wait until the end of the Seventies and the advent of Mark Knopfler to reinstate its popularity among guitarists. Knopfler's tasteful, clean-toned playing can be heard on Dire Straits' self-titled debut album from 1978, particularly on "Sultans Of Swing". The Stratocaster also played a part in the disco boom, with Nile Rodgers' playing on Chic's 1978 album *C'est Chic*, particularly on the track "Le Freak".

Ry Cooder's most commercial album *Bop Till You Drop*, from 1979, also includes some of his best playing, the slide guitar on "I Think It's Gonna Work Out Fine" being particularly impressive, again played on a Strat. Another subtle player, Jimmie Vaughan, may not be as famous as his younger brother Stevie Ray, but his playing with the Fabulous Thunderbirds reveals a tasteful and restrained guitarist. Vaughan masterfully interweaves rhythm and lead playing on "Wait On Time" from the Fabulous Thunderbirds' self-titled debut album (1979) and demonstrates how to play a slow blues on "Full-Time Lover".

Despite the attempts of punk to blow away all the old bands from the late Sixties and early Seventies, Pink Floyd continued to flourish, enjoying considerable success with its 1979 concept album *The Wall*. Dave Gilmour's Stratocaster playing was an integral part of the band's sound, as can be heard in his melodic playing in "Another Brick In The Wall, Part 2" and the awesome outro solo in "Comfortably Numb".

Derek and the Dominoes – Layla And Other Assorted Love Songs (RSO, 823 277-2)
Rory Gallagher – Live in Europe/Stage Struck (That's Original, TFOCD 20)
Deep Purple – Live in Japan (EMI, 7243 8 27726 2 0)
Robin Trower – Bridge of Sighs (Chrysalis, ACCD 1057)
Eagles – Hotel California (Asylum, 7559-60509-2)
Steve Miller Band – Fly Like An Eagle (Arcade, ARC 947102)
Dire Straits – Dire Straits (Vertigo, 800 051-2)

Chic – C'est Chic (Atlantic, 7567-81552-2)

Ry Cooder – Bop Till You Drop (Warner Bros, 7599-27398-2)

Fabulous Thunderbirds – The Fabulous Thunderbirds/What's The Word (Beat Goes On, BGOCD192)

Pink Floyd – The Wall (Harvest, CDS 7 46036 8)

THE EIGHTIES/NINETIES

The beginning of the Eighties saw a major advance in musical instrument technology which made synthesizers an affordable alternative to the electric guitar and spawned many synthesizer-based bands such as the Human League and Depeche Mode. Similar technological advances in electric guitars made effect pedals popular with many players and allowed new textures and sounds to be drawn from the instrument, as demonstrated by The Edge in U2 and Andy Summers in the Police. Despite these advances the classic Strat sound would enjoy its most successful period ever.

The mid Eighties saw a resurgence of interest in blues and 'roots' music with Stevie Ray Vaughan introducing many rock fans to blues and Robert Cray introducing blues to a more mainstream audience. This partly helped previously neglected blues artists such as John Lee Hooker and Buddy Guy to stage successful 'comebacks'. In the late Eighties heavy metal also made a strong comeback in the form of 'speed metal', with Metallica, Megadeth, Slayer and Anthrax inspiring many other sub-genres of metal.

On the rock guitar scene, a new generation of technically adept players continued in the style introduced by Eddie Van Halen and the success of Guns N' Roses prompted a resurgence of interest in early Seventies rock. The 'shredders' inspired by Eddie Van Halen and later by guitarists such as Steve Vai provoked an opposite reaction in the so-called 'grunge' bands of Pearl Jam, Soundgarden and Nirvana.

Unlike in the Sixties, when certain trends could be clearly identified in the music scene, in the Nineties we are seeing an increasingly diverse music scene with many different forms co-existing at the same time.

Although electric jazz guitarists have traditionally gone for thick, bassy sounds from non-Fender guitars, jazz great Miles Davis hired Stratocaster

Robert Cray

111

Stevie Ray Vaughan

player Mike Stern to play on the live album *We Want Miles*, from 1982. Stern's blend of rock and jazz guitar can be heard to great effect on the track "Jean-Pierre". Another highly talented but largely unknown 'fusion' player, Hiram Bullock, made a solo album in 1987, *Give It What U Got*, which shows an astonishing blend of funk, jazz and rock. A renowned session musician, Bullock guested on Sting's *Nothing Like The Sun* album in the same year, playing the solo on "Little Wing".

Rock man Stevie Ray Vaughan's debut *Texas Flood* (1983) was a mixture of blues and rock. Standout tracks from the album include the title track, "Pride And Joy", and the beautiful instrumental "Lenny", in which Vaughan coaxes a wide range of tones from his Strat and uses the vibrato arm to great effect. Many of the recent electric blues guitarists also use Strats, such as Robert Cray, Walter Trout, Ronnie Earl and Bonnie Raitt. Robert Cray's mainstream success occasionally means his guitar-playing takes a back seat, but his clean, stinging tone can be heard in a more bluesy context on the album he recorded with Albert Collins and Johnny Copeland in 1985, *Showdown*, particularly on the T-Bone Walker track "T-Bone Shuffle".

Increasing co-operation between guitarists and guitar-builders has given rise to signature model guitars which have advantages for both player and the instrument-maker. Robert Cray and Bon Jovi guitarist Richie Sambora are among the present generation of guitarists to have collaborated with Fender in this way. Sambora's Stratocaster playing can be heard on his 1991 solo album *Stranger In This Town*; Eric Clapton guests on the

track "Mr Bluesman".

Another guitarist to have a Stratocaster designed in his name is Swede Yngwie Malmsteen. Initially influenced by Ritchie Blackmore, Malmsteen almost single-handedly invented a new genre of 'neo-classical' rock guitar in 1984 with the album *Yngwie Malmsteen's Rising Force*. Malmsteen's technically astounding playing of blindingly fast arpeggios and harmonic minor scales recalls the violin playing of Paganini. Unfortunately, Malmsteen's songwriting doesn't match his guitar-playing.

Malmsteen embarked on a solo career after leaving rock band Alcatrazz, his replacement in Alcatrazz being Steve Vai. A technically proficient

Yngwie Malmsteen

and highly motivated player, Vai made a solo album, *Flex-Able,* in 1984 on which he largely played a couple of modified Strats, the main alterations being more powerful pickups and a locking vibrato system – the Fender company would later make similar changes to standard production Strats to accommodate players' changing needs. Vai's clean-toned Strat playing can be heard in the track "Call It Sleep".

Vai, a much-underrated guitarist with a unique and instantly recognizable guitar style, had previously played in Frank Zappa's band and can be heard as a rhythm guitarist on some of Zappa's 1988 album *Guitar*, an instrumental album dedicated to guitar solos – 32 of them! Zappa plays the majority of *Guitar* on a Stratocaster, either with a Custom Strat or the 'Hendrix Strat', rescued after

Hendrix burnt it in Miami in 1968. Another former member of Frank Zappa's band, Adrian Belew, who has also played with David Bowie, Talking Heads and King Crimson, is renowned for his ability to coax unusual sounds from his guitar and use them to musical effect. Belew's main instrument is a Fender Strat. Belew is on the Fender advisory board and his Strat playing can be heard on his solo album *Young Lions* (1990) with a noticeable Hendrix influence in the clean-toned guitar on the tracks "Heartbeat" and "Phone Call From The Moon".

Jeff Beck's *Guitar Shop* album (1989) finds Beck playing his unusually thick-necked signature model Strat and placing an emphasis on tone and texture rather than the flashy guitar playing he was associated with in the Sixties and Seventies. Beck comments on the haunting track "Where Were You": 'This piece was already in the Strat; it just had to be got out of it.' Another musician renowned for his attention to tone is Eric Johnson, whose 1990 solo album *Ah Via Musicom* again reveals a Hendrix influence, particularly in the evocative title track.

Richard Thompson's long and fruitful career is celebrated in the 1993 three-CD retrospective *Watching the Dark*. Thompson effortlessly blends traditional, folk influences with more esoteric influences, his main instrument being a clean-toned Strat. The retro rock sound of the Spin Doctors is based around Eric Schenkman, who plays a custom Strat designed after his 1965 sunburst Strat.

Miles Davis – We Want Miles (Columbia, COL469402 2)
Hiram Bullock – Give It What U Got (Atlantic Import, 7 81790-2)
Stevie Ray Vaughan & Double Trouble – Texas Flood (Epic, CD 460951)
Robert Cray, Albert Collins and Johnny Copeland – Showdown (Alligator, ALCD 4743)
Richie Sambora – Stranger In This Town (Phonogram, 848895)

Yngwie J Malmsteen – Yngwie Malmsteen's Rising Force (Polydor, 825 324-2)
Steve Vai – Flex-Able (Food for Thought, CDGRUB 3)
Frank Zappa – Guitar (Rykodisc, RCD 10079/10080)
Adrian Belew – Young Lions (Atlantic, 7567820992)
Jeff Beck – Guitar Shop (Epic, 463472 2)
Eric Johnson – Ah Via Musicom (Capitol, CDP 7 90517 2)
Richard Thompson – Watching The Dark (Hannibal, HNCD 5303)
Spin Doctors – Pocket Full Of Kryptonite (Sony, 468250 9)

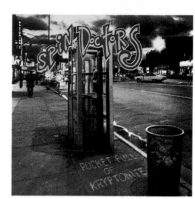

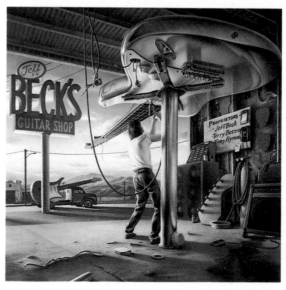

CHRONOLOGY

1909 Leo Fender is born on 10 August, near Anaheim, California.

1932 Rickenbacker, then called Ro-Pat-In, introduces the world's first production electric guitar, the "Frying Pan" Hawaiian model, designed by George Beauchamp and Paul Barth. The company also introduces the hollow body Electro Spanish, the first conventional electric guitar.

1935 Gibson develops its own electric lap steel, the EH-150. The following year it introduces its Electric Spanish ES-150. The first records featuring the electric guitar appear in this year.

1939 Leo Fender opens his radio shop, the Fender Radio Service, on Spadra Road, Fullerton, California.

1941 Les Paul, who has been experimenting with electric guitar designs, builds 'The Log', an early solid-body electric.

1943 Leo Fender builds his first solid-body electric guitar.

Leo Fender in 1979 **1945** Leo Fender and Doc Kauffman produce lap steel electrics under the K&F brand name.

1946 After Kauffman's departure, Leo Fender names his company the Fender Musical Instrument Co. His products are distributed by R&TEC in Santa Ana. R&TEC salesman Don Randall becomes heavily involved in the Fender operation.

1947 Paul Bigsby and Merle Travis design a solid-body electric guitar – they will both later claim that the guitar heavily influenced Leo's early designs.

1948 George Fullerton joins the Fender operation and assists Leo with his electric guitar designs.

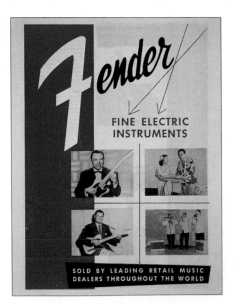

1950 Fender introduces the Esquire and the Broadcaster, now known as the world's first production solid-body guitar. A few Esquires were made in small numbers over the summer – the two-pickup Broadcaster is the first to make it into full production, around November.

1951 The Broadcaster is renamed the Telecaster. Fender introduces the radical twin-horn Precision Bass, which will influence the design of the Strat.

1952 Gibson decides to compete with the Telecaster and introduce their first solid body electric guitar, the Les Paul Model. Fender reorganizes their sales operation; now known as the Fender Sales Company, it will become a partnership between Don Randall and Leo Fender. Freddie Tavares joins to assist with design on the company's new guitar, which will become the Stratocaster.

1954 As rock 'n' roll starts to take hold, Fender introduces its new top-line electric, the Stratocaster. Eldon Shamblin, guitarist with Bob Wills, takes delivery of one of the first examples and uses it on the band's hit "Faded Love". Forrest White takes charge of Fender production.

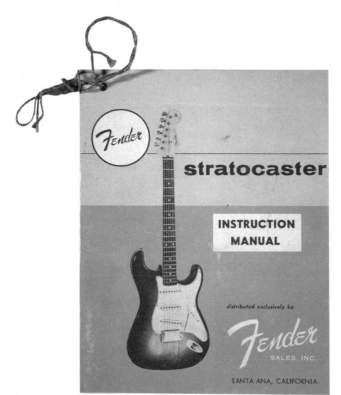

Fender instruction manual

Fender 1955 catalogue. (Throughout the years, the contemporary design of Fender's publicity material would help make their competitors look stuffy and old-fashioned)

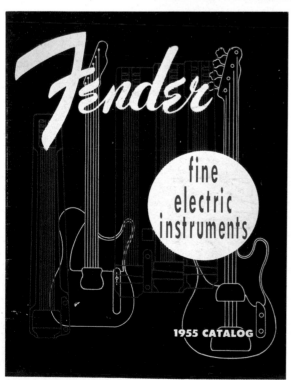

1957 Fender introduces its third professional electric six-string, the Jazzmaster. Although a well-designed guitar, it will never be as popular as the Strat or Tele. The Strat becomes more visible with the popularity of Buddy Holly and Chicago guitarists Otis Rush and Buddy Guy. Custom Colors are introduced.

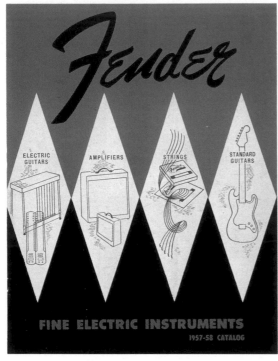

Above: 1957–58 catalogue

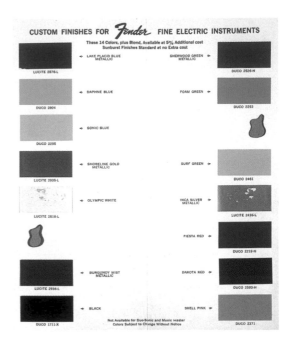

Right: 1966 Custom Color Chart – any color you want, including black

Fender's off-set electric six-string, the Jazzmaster

1960 Hank Marvin orders one of the first Stratocasters in Britain. He will inspire many British Invasion guitarists to take up the electric guitar, and help popularize the Strat in particular.

1965 On 4 January CBS buys the Fender company for $13 million.

1966 First CBS changes to the Strat include a new, larger, headstock design.

1967 Hendrix's masterful performance at Monterey in June helps break him in the US – and revives the fortunes of the Strat. Forrest White leaves Fender.

1969 Don Randall, President of CBS Musical Instruments, leaves the company.

1970 George Fullerton follows Randall's example and quits.

Right: The top-of-the-line Jaguar graces the cover of the 1963–64 catalogue. Above: 1968 catalogue

1971 New design features on the Strat include the 'bullet' truss rod adjustment and the infamous three-bolt neck method. The generally inferior quality of instruments of this period starts a fashion in 'pre-CBS' instruments.

1972 Ex-Fender employees Forrest White and Tom Walker start the Music Man company. Leo Fender will soon join them.

1977 Fender introduces the 'five-way' switch on the Strat.

'Bullet' truss rod Strat

1979 Dire Straits reach the UK singles charts with "Sultans Of Swing", recorded the previous year. It showcases the sound of the Fender Strat, and will help to engineer another revival in the guitar's fortunes. The company introduces its 'limited edition' 25th Anniversary models; early versions have a faulty finish which cracks within months, causing many to be returned to the factory.

1981 CBS brings in new management personnel to head the Fender company; Bill Schultz is Fender president, and Dan Smith takes charge of design.

1982 Fender Japan is established to sell Japanese-made guitars into the Oriental market.

1984 CBS decides to sell the Fender operation. Schultz and a group of investors complete a management buyout in February of the following year.

1985 Stevie Ray Vaughan is voted Best Electric Blues player by America's *Guitar Player* magazine. Vaughan is by now one of the Strat's major exponents, and helps to foster a new interest in blues. Other blues players such as Robert Cray are also highly visible Strat exponents.

1988 Fender produces the Eric Clapton Signature Strat, which proves to be a popular update of the Strat concept, and is soon followed by Robert Cray, Yngwie Malmsteen, Jeff Beck and Stevie Ray Vaughan signature models.

1991 Leo Fender dies on 21 March.

1994 To celebrate its 40th anniversary, Fender produces a limited edition run of replicas of the 1954 model Strat.

The 40th Anniversary Concert Edition

American Standard Stratocaster

GLOSSARY

ARCHTOP

Type of guitar body which, as its name suggests, features a top which is arched or domed, rather than flat, often with f-holes. These types of hollow body guitars were popularized by Gibson, and were the most common format for early electrics. Fender later introduced their own archtop electrics designed by Roger Rossmeisl; these were not particularly successful.

BLONDE

Blonde is a general term which refers to a light wood finish which became fashionable in the late Thirties. The Telecaster came in a blonde finish as standard; some early Strats are also seen in this color, most famously the one used by guitarist Mary Kaye, who was featured in early Fender catalogues.

BRIDGE

The guitar's bridge terminates the sounding length of the strings at the other end to the nut. The bridge of the Telecaster consists of three simple brass saddles. In the most common version of the Strat it is combined with a tremolo unit.

BRIDGE SADDLE

The saddle is the part of the bridge over which the strings pass. Adjustable saddles can be altered in height, for playing comfort, or forwards and backwards, for intonation adjustment. Different gauge strings require slightly different sounding lengths to play perfectly in tune – adjustable saddles therefore allow a wider range of string gauges to be accommodated.

BROADCASTER

The Broadcaster was Fender's first solid Spanish electric, produced in 1950. It would later be renamed the Telecaster, because Gretsch had a drumkit called Broadkaster.

'BULLET' TRUSS ROD

A type of truss rod adjustment introduced to Strats and Teles around 1971, and discontinued by 1981. Although perfectly efficient, it has become damned by its association with a period when Fender guitars are reputed to have reached their lowest point in terms of production and design quality.

CBS, PRE-CBS

The Columbia Broadcasting System company, which bought Fender on 1 January 1965 and sold it in February 1985. The term pre-CBS is often applied to Fender guitars made before the CBS takeover; these are generally thought to be of a higher quality than their successors.

CUSTOM COLOR

Up until late 1956 the standard finish for the Stratocaster was a two-tone sunburst. A small number of guitars were made in different colors, normally for artists who went direct to the factory. In late 1956 Fender started to offer a range of color options on all their guitars at a modest five percent surcharge – these were known as Custom Colors. Early Custom Color Strats fetch a premium price compared to their standard-finish counterparts because of their rarity.

CUTAWAY

This refers to the part of a guitar body which is removed to improve access to the neck. The Telecaster, for example, is a single cutaway guitar, while the Strat is a double cutaway guitar.

EQ, EQUALIZATION

EQ or equalization is basically a technical name for tone controls, which alter the amount of bass or treble in an electrical signal. Passive EQ, as found on the traditional Stratocaster, can only subtract a portion of a signal's sound – the passive tone control rolls off top, or treble. Leo Fender's later guitar designs for the Music Man brand featured Active EQ. Active EQ requires external power or batteries, and can add to the signal, actually increasing the amount of treble, middle or bass.

ESQUIRE

The one-pickup version of the Telecaster. A very small number of black and later blonde Esquires, without a truss rod, actually preceded the Broadcaster.

FLOYD ROSE

Type of tremolo system, developed from traditional Strat design by inventor of the same name. A Floyd Rose tremolo system uses locking saddles and fine tuners, usually in conjunction with a locking nut, to allow drastic pitch changes without tuning instability.

FULCRUM

Tremolo design, used on the Strat, in which the system pivots about a particular point; on the traditional version, the term denotes the six screws at the front of the bridge plate.

FULLERTON

Location of Leo Fender's first radio repair shop, and home of the Fender operation up to the time of its sale by CBS in 1985.

G&L

G&L were the last guitars designed by Leo Fender, with his long-time associate George Fullerton, from 1979. Although they would never attain the ubiquity of the early Fender models, many were efficient updates of basic Fender design concepts.

HEADSTOCK/HEAD

The headstock serves to hold the tuning machine heads. Fender guitars are synonymous with 'six-a-side' headstocks, which have all the machine heads in a straight line. This configuration allows the machine heads to be easily reached, while the 'straight string pull' improves tuning stability.

HUMBUCKING/HUMBUCKERS

Humbucking pickups, humbuckers for short, were perfected by Gibson's Seth Lover around 1955, and featured two coils wired in such a way as to reduce external hum and interference. They have a characteristic, fat sound. After he left Gibson, Seth Lover was recruited by Fender and started fitting his new version of the humbucking pickup to their guitars, notably the Telecaster Custom and Deluxe, in 1971. Modern 'stacked' or 'blade' humbuckers, as made by Seymour Duncan and other manufacturers, are intended to preserve the brightness of single coil designs, while rejecting interference.

IN-BETWEEN

The Stratocaster features three pickups, which on earlier models were selected by means of a three way switch; guitarists soon found that by lodging the switch in the 'in-between' position they could select two pickups at once; either neck and middle, or bridge and middle.

KLUSON

Type of machine head, supplied by the Chicago-based Kluson Manufacturing Company, fitted to Fender guitars until approximately 1967. They were subsequently replaced by tuners made by the German Schaller company, among others.

LACE SENSOR

Type of Fender pickup designed by Don Lace: its novel coil and magnet configuration features a very focused magnetic field which minimizes external interference. Lace Sensors come in various 'colors' which vary in output from a traditional single coil tone (Gold), to a more powerful version which offers the overdrive potential associated with

humbucking pickups (Red).

MUSIC MAN

Early Music Man guitars were designed and built for the company by Leo Fender's CLF operation from 1976, after his consultancy agreement with CBS expired. Music Man basses were among the first production instruments to feature active electronics, and were probably Leo Fender's most influential later design. Leo Fender parted company with Music Man in 1979, and went on to found G&L; the Music Man brand is now owned by the Ernie Ball string company.

PHASE, OUT OF PHASE

If two signals are 'in phase' then they perfectly coincide with each other, and reinforce each other's signal. If they are 'out of phase' then they cancel each other out. Combining two pickups on a guitar out of phase will therefore produce a sound that's weaker and tinnier than either pickup on its own. Guitarists often refer to a Strat's 'in-between' pickup selections as being out of phase, which is not the case. However, there are subtle differences between the signals detected by both pickups, which contribute to the distinctive sound.

PICKUP

Device which converts string vibration into an electrical signal. Fender are normally associated with single coil pickups.

SCALE LENGTH

This is effectively the sounding length of a guitar string, or the distance from nut to bridge saddle. Fender are associated with a 25 ½ inch (648mm) scale length as on the Strat, although models such as the Duo-Sonic and Jaguar featured shorter scale lengths.

SINGLE COIL

Single coil pickups, as fitted to the original Stratocaster, consist of a set of slug magnets sur-rounded by one coil of copper wire wound on a bobbin. They are simple to make, offer a characteristic bright and clear sound, but are susceptible to interference.

SKUNK STRIPE

The first versions of the Stratocaster and Telecaster featured a truss rod which was installed from the back of the neck. The necessary rout was filled with a darker wood, often walnut, which is referred to as a skunk stripe.

SQUIER

Trade name owned by Fender, initially used for guitar strings and from 1983, applied to Stratocasters built in Japan and, from 1988, Korea.

SUNBURST

Sunburst was the standard finish for the Stratocaster from launch. Early Stratocasters are often referred to as 'two-tone' because of their two-tone sunburst finish, in which the black at the outside of the guitar body fades into the natural yellow wood color at the center. In 1958 the Strat changed to a three-tone sunburst which fades from black into red into yellow; however, on early three-tone Strats the red dye used faded on exposure to light, so that over time they changed to a two-tone appearance!

TREMOLO

Variation in volume. Often a misnomer for vibrato as in 'tremolo arm', or 'tremolo bridge'. As these affect pitch and not volume, they should really be termed 'vibrato arm' or 'vibrato bridge', but Fender itself has helped to standardize this misnomer.

VIBRATO

Variation in pitch. For guitar purposes this refers to altering the pitch of a string by moving the strings sideways, or by rolling the finger over the string.

KEY PEOPLE

CARSON, BILL
Western Swing guitarist who was an important consultant in the design of the Stratocaster. He later joined Fender full-time in the sales department.

FENDER, LEO
Inventor of the Fender Strat, and all other Fender guitars until 1966. Leo Fender later designed guitars sold under the Music Man and G&L marques. His Fender amplifier designs were also incredibly influential: early Marshall and Mesa Boogie amplifiers were derived from Fender designs.

FULLERTON, GEORGE
George Fullerton joined the Fender company in 1948, and was Leo Fender's major assistant in the design of the Telecaster. He stayed with Fender until 1970, and would later team up with Leo Fender in the CLF and G&L companies.

RANDALL, DON
Originally salesman for R&TEC, the first distributor of Fender products, Don Randall later became head of the Fender Sales Organization, in which he and Leo Fender were partners. Randall became President of CBS Musical Instruments after the CBS takeover, but left the company in 1969 to found Randall Electric Instruments.

TAVARES, FREDDIE
Musician who joined the Fender company in 1953 and was Leo Fender's premier collaborator in the design of the Stratocaster. Tavares was involved in many subsequent Fender designs and remained with the company until the early Eighties.

WHITE, FORREST
Head of production for all Fender products, Forrest White joined Fender in 1954. He left the company in 1967.

INDEX

ACKNOWLEDGEMENTS
The authors would like to thank the following for their assistance in the production of this book:
Ivor Arbiter; Sarah Ball; William Burdett-Coutts; Bill Carson; Lee Dickson; all at Fender; George Fullerton; Sue Hanson; Norman Harris of Norman's Rare Guitars; Carolyn Jennings; Senji Kasuya; Mel Kay; Robb Lawrence; Jim Lewis; Jeff Lynne; Royston Mayo; Nordoff-Robbins; John Page; PMI; Stuart Prebble; Don Randall; Alan Rogan; Bill Schultz; Brian Shepherd; Dan Smith; Chris Trigg of Vintage & Rare; Paul Trynka; Forrest White; *Young Guitar Magazine* Japan; Lenny Zakatak; Rick Zsigmond of Fat Rick's Emporium; and all of the artists and their managements.

PHOTOGRAPH CREDITS
SchemeGlobal Productions Limited would like to thank the following sources for their kind permission to reproduce the pictures in this book:
Ace Records: 106 (bottom); **Bill Carson**: 22, 25, 27; **Andrew Catlin**: 99; **Steve Catlin**: 58, 61, 117, 118; **Charly Records**: 108 (tr); **EMI**: 107; **Fender Musical Instruments**: 12, 13, 32, 37, 38, 39, 63, 64, 65, 66; **James Cumpsty/Guitar Magazine**: 82, 116; **Robert Knight**: 83; **Robb Lawrence**: 27, 33; **London Features International**: 84 (bl), 104 (b), 108 (tl), 109 (tr), 110 (tl), 110 (bl), LFI/Michael Ochs Archive 8 (tr), 70 (bl), 105 (br); **MCA**: 106; **Steve Miller**: 92; **John Peck**: 81; **Don Randall**: 24; **Rex Features**: 6 (cl), 71 (c); **Stephen Sandon**: 96. **Fin Costello/SchemeGlobal Limited**: 2, 5, 6 (guitar body and neck), 7, 9, 11 (Ray and neck), 15, 23, 28, 29, 30, 31, 33 (catalogue), 35, 36, 45, 46, 47, 48 (neck), 49, 51, 52, 54, 55, 62, 66 (except Sunburst guitar), 69 (neck), 70 (headstock), 87 (hotel), 104 (neck), 114 (catalogue), 115, 116 (catalogue), 17 (catalogue), 119, 121, 123; **Minhinnett & Young/SchemeGlobal Limited**: 10, 14, 20, 42, 43, 48, 53, 60, 72, 74, 78, 79, 80, 86, 87, 88, 102, 113; **Pete Vernon/SchemeGlobal Limited**: 11, 67, 77, 93, 94. **Stephen Sandon**: 96; **Steve Stickler**: 100; **Forrest White**: 16; **William Hames/Young Guitar Magazine**: 50, 56, 57, 59; **Robert Zuckerman**: 90, 112.
Every effort has been made to acknowledge correctly and contact the source and/or copyright holder of each picture, and Carlton Books Limited apologizes for any unintentional errors or omissions, which will be corrected in future editions of this book.